"The "Connoisseur" is above all an individual. An authority on hotels, with a wealth of experience; his opinions have acted as a touchstone for travellers throughout the world.

A subjective judge of the quintessential British hotel, Connoisseur distills the essence of each establishment into an easily assimilated guide for the discerning.

As the title suggests, this is a "personal" choice of some of the more interesting hotels in Great Britain.
Nearly all are owner operated. They have not been selected by committee or some anonymous collection of "so-called" inspectors. They are individual establishments selected by an individual ... myself!

I hope you will like this selection. I have tried to choose hotels run by "human" beings. Which is why you will find some of the "grand" hotels have been omitted.
Their owners are very often as unwelcoming and as cheerless as the hotels they command.
I like to recommend establishments where the phrase "a warm welcome" is not just a cliche, but a reality.

Published by
CHARISMA PUBLICATIONS

Copright © 1993
CHARISMA PUBLICATIONS 2ND EDITION

ISBN 0 9518181 1 2

Published by
CHARISMA PUBLICATIONS
12 Victoria Quay, Malpas, Truro, Cornwall TR1 1SO

Production management by
FIELD PUBLISHING SERVICES
Field House, North Street, Martock, Somerset TA12 6EH

Typeset by
FLAYDEMOUSE

Maps by
OXFORD CARTOGRAPHERS

Printed in England by
JENSEN PRESS (SW) LTD
4 Bofors Park, Artillery Road, Yeovil, Somerset

Front cover: Farlam Hall, Brampton (Page 36)

How to locate a Hotel

1. First look at the maps at the beginning of England/Scotland/Wales. If I am featuring a hotel the place name will be highlighted in bold typeface. Follow along the top of the pages, which are arranged alphabetically, until you arrive at the location.

2. If you already have the name of a hotel and wish to know if it is included, turn to the index at the back of the book. Hotels are listed in alphabetical order.

In some cases where hotels are located close to major towns, they may be shown under that town with the exact location shown in brackets.
Example: BATH (Chelwood).

PRICE GUIDE: This quote is based on an overnight SINGLE and DOUBLE. Normally this is for Bed & Breakfast but sometimes if dinner is included it will be indicated in brackets: i.e. (includes dinner)

NOTE: The prices quoted above are for a one night stay only, but most of the establishments in this guide offer reductions for stays of two or more nights. Also, do enquire about special bargain breaks.

"Unlike me, my Rolex never needs a rest."

Wherever his travels may take him, Placido Domingo takes a series of green bound books. Into these he writes his engagements three years ahead; such are the demands of the major Opera Houses of the world on the man acclaimed as possibly the greatest living tenor.

Placido Domingo has committed some eighty different operatic roles to memory. He believes this daunting repertoire is necessary to attract the widest possible audience.

For this is his driving ambition: to help more people, all over the world, enjoy and appreciate the music that he loves.

In recent years, Domingo has presented a live video performance of 'La Boheme' to an audience outside Covent Garden.

He provoked a rapturous ovation in China (until then, Chinese audiences seldom even applauded). And a legendary curtain call in Barcelona lasted one hour and fifty minutes. "It would have been easier," Placido has said, "to sing the opera all over again."

Over and above this punishing schedule, Placido has been appointed President of the European Youth Opera and has renewed his interest in conducting.

As a student at the Mexico City Conservatoire, this was his main study. Now Domingo can bring all the experience of his singing career to bear on his conducting. "The operatic conductor is like a Roman charioteer," he says. "He has a hundred horses in the pit. And he has to control them all."

To keep up with these ever-increasing demands on his time Placido Domingo, the Ambassador of Opera, relies on his Rolex. "This watch is perfect for me," he says, "because, unlike me, it never needs a rest. You could say it's one of my favourite instruments."

ROLEX
of Geneva

5

Contents

Use the order forms at the back of the book to obtain your personal copy.

The Ideal gift for a friend, relative or business associate.

If you know of an individual Hotel of quality, not already included, please write to "Connoisseur" at Charisma Publications, A4 Shirley Towers, Vale Hill Road, Torquay TQ1 2BY and, if space permits, I would be happy to consider it for the 1994 edition.

Introduction to England

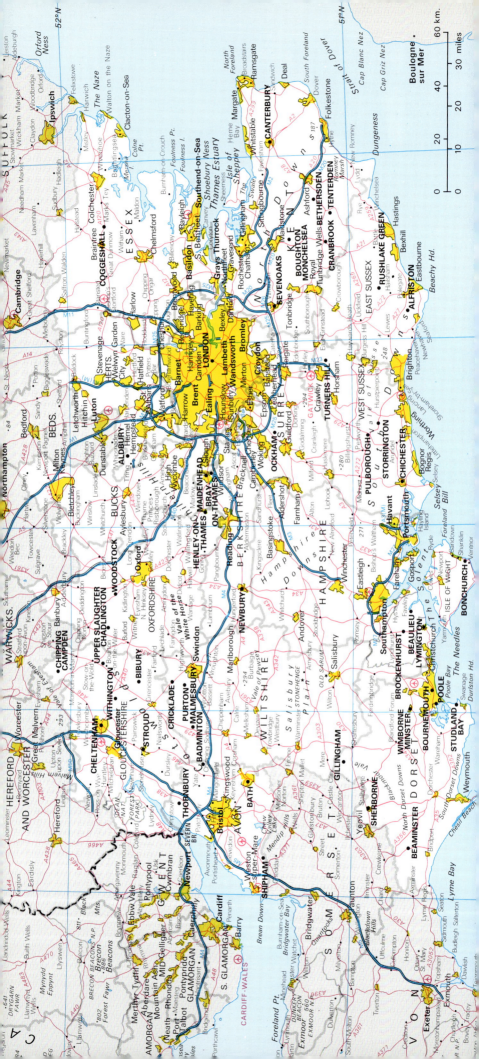

Stocks Country House Hotel

Aldbury, Nr Tring, Hertfordshire HP23 5RX
Tel: 044285 341 · Fax: 044285 253

This elegant hotel is situated in tranquil grounds surrounded by its own magnificent golf course, at present under construction and due for completion by 1994. This ex training ground for Bunny girls is now a comfortable hotel. Food is excellent, well prepared and presented and served in the delightful Tapestry Restaurant. Great care has been taken over the furnishings and fabrics in the pleasing bedrooms. There are too many leisure facilities to list but these include: riding, four all weather tennis courts, pool and gymnasium etc. Do enquire about corporate packages.

OPEN: **All year**
NO. ROOMS: **18** EN SUITE **17**
ROOM TELEPHONES: **Yes** TV IN ROOMS: **Yes**
PETS: **No** CHILDREN: **Yes**
DISABLED: **Unsuitable**

SWIMMING POOL: **Outdoor Heated**
CONFERENCE FACILITIES:
Business Meetings up to 65
PRICE GUIDE:
SINGLE: **£70** DOUBLE: **£90**

White Lodge Country House Hotel

Sloe Lane, Alfriston, East Sussex BN26 5UR
Tel: 0323 870265 · Fax: 0323 870284

Situated in a commanding position within its own 5 acres of grounds overlooking the Sussex Downs, this interesting hotel is owned and run by Don and Maureen Denyer. Elaborate French furnishings, heavy drapes and crystal chandeliers adorn public rooms whilst each bedroom is individually designed with a host of thoughtful extras. The house boasts many fine pieces like a superb 120 year old Grand Piano, original paintings and fine sculpted studies. With its reputation for imaginative food and fine wines, White Lodge is a wise choice whatever the occasion.

OPEN: *All year*
NO. ROOMS: *20* EN SUITE *20*
ROOM TELEPHONES: *Yes* TV IN ROOMS: *Yes*
PETS: *No* CHILDREN: *Yes*
DISABLED: *Yes*
LOCATION: *One mile from roundabout on A27*

SWIMMING POOL/HEALTH CLUB: *No*
CONFERENCE FACILITIES:
Small Business Meetings up to 16
PRICE GUIDE:
SINGLE: *£55/£65* DOUBLE: *£83/£121*

Rothay Manor

Rothay Bridge, Ambleside, Cumbria LA22 0EH
Tel: 05394 33605 · Fax: 05394 33607

Perhaps the adjective that best sums up this small Regency style hotel is - elegant. Public rooms and bedrooms are all - elegant. Open fires, fresh flowers, comfortable settees and period furniture blend to make your stay memorable. Bedrooms are supremely stylish with fresh appealing design and decor. Rothay Manor has an international reputation for the quality of its food, established over many years. Imaginative dishes are presented with great flair in an elegant (there goes that word again!) atmosphere of fine crystal, crisp napiery, candle-light and fresh flowers. Owned and managed by the Nixon family.

OPEN: *2nd week February to early January*
NO. ROOMS: *15* EN SUITE *15*
ROOM TELEPHONES: *Yes* TV IN ROOMS: *Yes*
PETS: *No* CHILDREN: *Yes*
DISABLED: *Yes*
LOCATION: *Follow Coniston signs (A593)*

SWIMMING POOL/HEALTH CLUB: *No*
CONFERENCE FACILITIES: *No*
PRICE GUIDE: SINGLE: *£74*
DOUBLE: *£105/£118*

Callow Hall

Mappleton Road, Ashbourne, Derbyshire DE6 2AA
Tel: 0335 43403 · Fax: 0335 43624

As soon as you enter this mellow old house, it is obvious that owners David and Dorothy Spencer really care for their guests comfort. All the charming bedrooms are individually designed and have superb bathrooms with most attractive fittings ... and plumbing to match! David Spencer heads the kitchen team who produce succulent dishes and goes to extraordinary lengths to personally obtain the finest produce. It is reassuring to find that old fashioned standards of courtesy and service live on at Callow Hall.

OPEN: ***All year***
NO. ROOMS: ***12*** EN SUITE ***12***
ROOM TELEPHONES: ***Yes*** TV IN ROOMS: ***Yes***
PETS: ***By Arrangement*** CHILDREN: ***Yes***
DISABLED: ***Unsuitable***
LOCATION: ***Turn off A515 opposite Bowling Green Pub then first right***

SWIMMING POOL/HEALTH CLUB: ***No***
CONFERENCE FACILITIES:
Small Business Meetings up to 24
PRICE GUIDE:
SINGLE: ***£65/£80*** DOUBLE: ***£87.50/£115***

Holne Chase Hotel

Two Bridges Road, Ashburton, Devon TQ13 7NS
Tel: 03643 471 · Fax: 03643 453

This former hunting lodge has the twin advantages of easy accessibility from the main A38 road yet at the same time is totally secluded and could be miles from the "madding throng". Owned and operated by the Bromage family the atmosphere is relaxed, bring your child, your wellies and your dog, you will be welcome. Open fires burn in public rooms, bedrooms are pleasing and well equipped and you will enjoy good food whilst contemplating the superb views. For fishermen the hotel has over a mile of water on the River Dart, whilst for golfers there are 12 courses within 25 miles of the hotel.

OPEN: **All year**
NO. ROOMS: **14** EN SUITE **14**
ROOM TELEPHONES: **Yes** TV IN ROOMS: **Yes**
PETS: **Yes** CHILDREN: **Yes**
DISABLED: **Yes**
LOCATION: **Three miles north of Ashburton**

SWIMMING POOL/HEALTH CLUB: **No**
CONFERENCE FACILITIES:
Small Business Meetings up to 25
PRICE GUIDE:
SINGLE: **£59** DOUBLE: **£90/£120**

Tytherleigh Cot Hotel

Chardstock, Axminster, Devon EX13 7BN
Tel: 0460 21170 · Fax: 0460 21291

Friendly owners, Frank and Pat Grudgings will make you most welcome at their 14th century grade II listed complex of luxury bedrooms, air-conditioned restaurant, conference room and leisure facilities. Bedrooms are the last word in sybaritic self-indulgence, furnished with great flair using fine fabrics and quality appointments. Suites have superb bathrooms with double Jacuzzies, 4-posters, half testers and inglenook fireplaces. Overlooking the fountain and lily pond you can enjoy English and French cuisine in the elegant Conservatory Restaurant.

OPEN: **All year**
NO. ROOMS: **20** EN SUITE **20**
ROOM TELEPHONES: **Yes** TV IN ROOMS: **Yes**
PETS: **By arrangement** CHILDREN: **Over 12**
DISABLED: **Unsuitable**
LOCATION: **Off A358 Chard – Axminster road**

SWIMMING POOL: **Outdoor Heated**
CONFERENCE FACILITIES:
Small Business Meetings up to 20
PRICE GUIDE:
SINGLE: **£53.75/£58** DOUBLE: **£91/£108**

Petty France Hotel

Dunkirk, Badminton, Avon GL9 1AF
Tel: 0454 238361 · Fax: 0454 238768

This pretty hotel nestles in its own peaceful gardens. Built of warm Cotswold stone, it is ideally located for visiting the Severn Valley, Forest of Dean and the Roman city of Bath, whilst the beautiful Westonbirt Arboretum with its magnificent specimen trees is nearby. Charming public rooms open off one another, in Summer there are fresh flowers from the garden and in Winter log fires bid you welcome. Good food and comfortable bedrooms ensure your stay at Petty France will be an enjoyable experience.

OPEN: *All year*
NO. ROOMS: *20* EN SUITE *20*
ROOM TELEPHONES: *Yes* TV IN ROOMS: *Yes*
PETS: *Yes* CHILDREN: *Yes*
DISABLED: *Yes*
LOCATION: *5 miles north of M4 exit 18 on A46*

SWIMMING POOL/HEALTH CLUB: *No*
CONFERENCE FACILITIES:
Small Business Meetings up to 14
PRICE GUIDE: SINGLE: *£59/£70*
DOUBLE: *£85/£105 (inc Cont Bkfast)*

The Glebe at Barford

Church Street, Barford, Warwickshire CV35 8BS
Tel: 0926 624218 · Fax: 0926 624625

If this stunningly stylish hotel with its elegant decor becomes as popular as it deserves to be, it will not be "Warwickshire's best kept secret" for long! All bedrooms are beautifully designed and furnished with soft pastel fabrics, exquisite bathrooms have marble floors as does the air-conditioned Cocktail Bar. Food is delicious and excellent value for money. There is a fine Leisure Club and superb high-tech facilities for the businessman. Staff are attentive and courteous.

OPEN: **All year**
NO. ROOMS: **41** EN SUITE **41**
ROOM TELEPHONES: **Yes** TV IN ROOMS: **Yes**
PETS: **By arrangement** CHILDREN: **Yes**
DISABLED: **Yes**
LOCATION: **On A429 south of Warwick**

SWIMMING POOL/HEALTH CLUB: **Yes**
CONFERENCE FACILITIES:
Theatre Style up to 130
PRICE GUIDE:
SINGLE: **£90** DOUBLE: **£105**

Halmpstone Manor

Bishops Tawton, Barnstaple, N. Devon EX32 0EA
Tel: 0271 830321 · Fax: 0271 830826

Jane and Charles Stanbury will welcome you most warmly to their highly individual and ultra charming small Manor set in the heart of rural Devonshire. Romantic bedrooms have 4-posters, coronet beds and superb bathrooms. There is an atmospheric Dining Room in which to enjoy creative cooking, log fires in winter. Devonshire Cream Teas in Summer. I am sure the magic of Halmpstone will work its spell on you ... it did on me!

OPEN: ***All year***
NO. ROOMS: **5** EN SUITE **5**
ROOM TELEPHONES: ***Yes*** TV IN ROOMS: ***Yes***
PETS: ***Yes*** CHILDREN: ***No***
DISABLED: ***Unsuitable***
LOCATION: ***Take A377 to Bishops Tawton and turn opposite BP station.***

SWIMMING POOL/HEALTH CLUB: ***No***
CONFERENCE FACILITIES:
Small Business Meetings up to 10
PRICE GUIDE:
SINGLE: **£70** DOUBLE: **£80/£130**

Fischers Baslow Hall

Claver Road, Baslow, Derbyshire DE4 1RR
Tel: 0246 583259

Owned and operated by Max and Susan Fischer, this small very personal hotel with its charming individual bedrooms, is a monument to good food and fine wines. No condiments appear on the tables in the elegant Dining Room. Max prides himself on producing dishes of such perfection that they are not necessary. "Food fit for the Gods" might well be the slogan here. Classic dishes, traditional dishes or roasts, are all presented with great flair and imagination to produce a memorable gastronomic experience.

OPEN: **All year**
NO. ROOMS: **6** EN SUITE **6**
ROOM TELEPHONES: **Yes** TV IN ROOMS: **Yes**
PETS: **No** CHILDREN: **Yes**
DISABLED: **Unsuitable**

SWIMMING POOL/HEALTH CLUB: **No**
CONFERENCE FACILITIES:
Small Business Meetings up to 14
PRICE GUIDE: SINGLE: **£62.50**
DOUBLE: **£87.50/£107.50**

LOCATION: **Off A623 signed Stockport and then Hall is on right leaving town**

Pheasant Inn

Bassenthwaite Lake, Cockermouth, Cumbria
Tel: 07687 76234 · Fax: 07687 76002

The Perfect example of a genuine Lakeland Inn. Mellow, atmospheric lounges and bars, log fires, oak beams and truly delightful bedrooms are light, airy and immaculate, whilst good English food is served in the charming Dining Room. Originating from a 200 year old farm, the Inn is under the personal supervision of Mr & Mrs Barrington Wilson, who are both Cumbrians. If you are seeking character and tranquillity you could hardly better the Pheasant, Lakeland Inn "par excellence"

OPEN: **All year**
NO. ROOMS: **20** EN SUITE **20**
ROOM TELEPHONES: **No** TV IN ROOMS: **No**
PETS: **No** CHILDREN: **Over 12**
DISABLED: **Unsuitable**
LOCATION: **Just off A66 seven miles North West of Keswick**

SWIMMING POOL/HEALTH CLUB:
No
CONFERENCE FACILITIES:
No
PRICE GUIDE: SINGLE: **£52** DOUBLE: **£90**

Hunstrete House

Hunstrete, Chelwood, Nr Bristol, Avon BS18 4NS
Tel: 0761 490490 · Fax: 0761 490732

This graceful house has long enjoyed an enviable reputation as one of the finest country house hotels in the Bath area. That reputation continues today. Classically proportioned public rooms have antiques, paintings, fresh flowers, pottery, porcelain, and log fires. The Dining Room looks out onto an Italianate Courtyard filled with flowers, and presents creative cuisine in an atmosphere of charm and elegance. Bedrooms are quite lovely and generally the atmosphere is more that of a luxurious home. Hunstrete is surrounded by an idyllic English garden.

OPEN: **All year**
NO. ROOMS: **24** EN SUITE **24**
ROOM TELEPHONES: **Yes** TV IN ROOMS: **Yes**
PETS: **No** CHILDREN: **No**
DISABLED: **Unsuitable**
LOCATION: **From A39 take A368 at Marksbury to Hunstrete**

SWIMMING POOL: **Outdoor Heated**
CONFERENCE FACILITIES:
Small Business Meetings up to 24
PRICE GUIDE:
SINGLE: **£95** DOUBLE: **£150**

Holly Lodge

8 Upper Oldfield Park, Bath, Avon BA2 3JZ
Tel: 0225 424042 · Fax: 0225 481138

This charming Victorian Town House commands panoramic views of the city from its elevated position. A rare find. This charming oasis is delightfully furnished with individually designed bedrooms and superb bathrooms. Elegant and stylish. Holly Lodge is owned and operated with meticulous attention to detail by Carroll Settick and George Hall on a room and breakfast basis. Home baking can be enjoyed in the appealing breakfast room with its yellow and green decor and white wicker chairs. Furnished with antiques, this immaculate establishment makes a pleasant baser when visiting the Roman City of Bath.

OPEN: **All year**
NO. ROOMS: **6** EN SUITE **6**
ROOM TELEPHONES: **Yes** TV IN ROOMS: **Yes**
PETS: **No** CHILDREN: **Yes**
DISABLED: **Yes**
LOCATION: **Off the A367 Exeter Road**

SWIMMING POOL/HEALTH CLUB: **No**
CONFERENCE FACILITIES:
No
PRICE GUIDE:
SINGLE: **£50/£60** DOUBLE: **£65/£85**

Apsley House Hotel

Newbridge Hill, Bath, Avon BA1 3PT
Tel: 0225 336966 · Fax: 0225 425462

This small William IV period house is quietly located near the centre of this historically important city. Offering the kind of service possible only in a privately owned establishment, Apsley House is run in a very personal way by Mr & Mrs Davidson. Comfortable bedrooms are individual in design and equal in comfort. In the elegant surroundings of the dining room, guests can enjoy Mrs Davidson's food whilst drinking in the tranquillity of the delightful garden.

OPEN: **All year**
NO. ROOMS: **7** EN SUITE **7**
ROOM TELEPHONES: **Yes** TV IN ROOMS: **Yes**
PETS: **No** CHILDREN: **Over 14**
DISABLED: **Unsuitable**
LOCATION: **On the A431 Kelston Road 1 mile from Queen's Square**

SWIMMING POOL/HEALTH CLUB: **No**
CONFERENCE FACILITIES:
Small Business Meetings
PRICE GUIDE:
SINGLE: **From £60** DOUBLE: **From £80**

The Bridge House Hotel

Beaminster, Dorset DT8 3AY
Tel: 0308 862200 · Fax: 0308 863700

The old market town of Beaminster at the heart of Thomas Hardy country is an ideal centre for touring the beautiful Dorset countryside. Bridge House, a former 13th century priests house makes a comfortable base for this purpose, with its inglenook fireplaces in which log fires burn, cosy beamed lounge, candle-lit dining room and pleasant bedrooms. A feature of this old property is the delightful walled garden and nearby are numerous important houses, gardens and golf courses.

OPEN: *All year*
NO. ROOMS: *14* EN SUITE *14*
ROOM TELEPHONES: *Yes* TV IN ROOMS: *Yes*
PETS: *Yes* CHILDREN: *No*
DISABLED: *Yes*
LOCATION: *200 Yards from Town Centre*

SWIMMING POOL/HEALTH CLUB: *No*
CONFERENCE FACILITIES:
Small Business Meetings up to 12-14
PRICE GUIDE:
SINGLE: *£31/£60* DOUBLE: *£56/£92*

The Montagu Arms Hotel

Beaulieu, Hampshire SO42 7ZL
Tel: 0590 612324 · Fax: 0590 612188

This creeper clad listed hotel has all the charm of a bygone era with its oak panelling, beamed ceilings and log fires. The delightful Restaurant looks onto terraced gardens and has a considerable reputation for its food. The hotel has its own bakery, the croissants at Breakfast were the best I have tasted. Imaginatively designed bedrooms have individual decor. Guests have use of the superb Health Complex at sister hotel Carey's Manor (see under Brockenhurst). Notable visitors to the hotel are the herds of wild ponies which throng the streets.

OPEN: ***All year***
NO. ROOMS: **24** EN SUITE **24**
ROOM TELEPHONES: **Yes** TV IN ROOMS: **Yes**
PETS: **Yes** CHILDREN: **Over 5**
DISABLED: **Unsuitable**

SWIMMING POOL/HEALTH CLUB: **No**
CONFERENCE FACILITIES:
Small Business Meetings up to 30
PRICE GUIDE:
SINGLE: **£70** DOUBLE: **£95/£165**

The Blue Bell Hotel

Market Place, Belford, Northumberland NE70 7NE
Tel: 0668 213543 · Fax: 0668 213787

A small gem of an Inn whose modest exterior belies the quite lovely decor within. All bedrooms are most appealing, every one of them different but all equally stylish and comfortable. There is an elegant lounge, a Garden Restaurant laid with fine crystal and candle-light and for more simple meals a Buttery. Overlooking a lovely garden the Blue Bell is a charming and individual place in an area where good hotels are thin on the ground.

OPEN: **All year**
NO. ROOMS: **17** EN SUITE **17**
ROOM TELEPHONES: **Yes** TV IN ROOMS: **Yes**
PETS: **By arrangement**
CHILDREN: **By arrangement**
LOCATION: **Off A1 in centre of village**

DISABLED: **Yes**
SWIMMING POOL/HEALTH CLUB: **No**
CONFERENCE FACILITIES: **Yes**
PRICE GUIDE:
SINGLE: **£40** DOUBLE: **£72/£82**

Little Hodgeham

Bull Lane, Bethersden, Ashford, Kent TN26 3HE
Tel: 0233 850323

The archetypal English country cottage. A rose bowered picture postcard 500 years old Tudor gem, set in a myriad scented dream of an English Garden, a riot of colour surrounding a gurgling stream, flood-lit as evening drops into night. Inside, more colour, gleaming antiques, log fires and cosy chairs. You eat Erica Wallaces succulent food seated at a single oval table laid with the finest crystal, exquisite bone china and elegant silver. Pretty bedrooms, one with 4-poster, are artistically colour co-ordinated. Not a hotel this, but one of the most charming and individual establishments in this book.

OPEN: **Mid March to September 1st**
NO. ROOMS: **3** EN SUITE **3**
ROOM TELEPHONES: **No** TV IN ROOMS: **No**
PETS & CHILDREN: **By arrangement**
DISABLED: **Unsuitable**

SWIMMING POOL: **Outdoor**
CONFERENCE FACILITIES: **No**
PRICE GUIDE:
SINGLE: **£58 (incl Dinner)**
DOUBLE: **£94 (incl Dinner)**

LOCATION: **Turn off A28 at Bull Pub, Bethersden, two miles towards Smarden**

The Swan Hotel

Bibury, Gloucestershire GL7 5NW
Tel: 0285 740695 · Fax: 0285 740473

Anyone familiar with this creeper clad 17th century hotel prior to its take over in 1991 by Elizabeth Hayles and Alex Furtek, will be staggered as I was at the magical transformation they have worked. Highlights include stunning, imaginatively designed interiors, open fires, delightful bedrooms, superb bathrooms, three with Jacuzzies, and an elegant dining room serving the finest of food and wines in an atmosphere of fine crystal. There is an interesting Brasserie, and Oh Yes, a Baby Grand Piano played by a phantom pianist!

OPEN: ***All year except Xmas & New Year***
NO. ROOMS: ***18*** EN SUITE ***18***
ROOM TELEPHONES: ***Yes*** TV IN ROOMS: ***Yes***
PETS: ***In Kennels*** CHILDREN: ***Yes***
DISABLED: ***Yes***

SWIMMING POOL/HEALTH CLUB: ***No***
CONFERENCE FACILITIES:
Small Business Meetings up to 12
PRICE GUIDE:
SINGLE: ***From £100*** DOUBLE: ***£120-£160***

Norton Place Hotel

180 Lifford Lane, Kings Norton, Birmingham B30 3NT
Tel: 021-433 5656 · Fax: 021-433 3048

This dazzling oasis offers un-paralleled standards of comfort, as one guest put it. "I thought I had died and arrived in Heaven". The Palace of Brunei and Nat. Portrait Gallery share the same craftspeople. Stunning bedrooms are sublimely luxurious with fabulous marble bathrooms with gold accessories. Concealed T.V.s and videos rise electronically at the touch of a button. Stained glass, original oils, marble fireplaces and exquisite fabrics and furnishings grace each room. Superb cuisine is served in the elegant Lombard Room dressed with fresh flowers and fine crystal. A pianist plays at dinner.

OPEN: **All year**
NO. ROOMS: **10** EN SUITE **10**
ROOM TELEPHONES: **Yes** TV IN ROOMS: **Yes**
PETS: **In Kennels** CHILDREN: **Over 10**
DISABLED: **Yes**

SWIMMING POOL/HEALTH CLUB: **No**
CONFERENCE FACILITIES:
Theatre Style up to 150
PRICE GUIDE:
SINGLE: **£90/£225** DOUBLE: **£99/£250**

LOCATION: **Exit M42 at Jcn 3 & take A435 to Kings Norton following Patrick Collection signs**

The Devonshire Arms

Bolton Abbey, Skipton, N. Yorkshire BD23 6AJ
Tel: 0756 710441 · Fax: 0756 710564

Exceptionally high standards apply at this beautifully arranged hotel, the decor and exquisite furnishings being the work of the Duchess of Devonshire. The highly individual bedrooms are idiosyncratic with unique themes (seven with 4-posters), even to a room specially designed for the ladies! The enchanting Burlington Restaurant is the setting for superlative food and wines. For businessmen every conceivable support facility is available in the Cavendish Suite.

OPEN: **All year**
NO. ROOMS: **40** EN SUITE **40**
ROOM TELEPHONES: **Yes** TV IN ROOMS: **Yes**
PETS: **Yes** CHILDREN: **Yes**
DISABLED: **Yes**
LOCATION: **Off A59 five miles from Skipton towards Harrogate**

SWIMMING POOL/HEALTH CLUB: **No**
CONFERENCE FACILITIES:
Theatre Style up to 150
PRICE GUIDE:
SINGLE: **£78/£85** DOUBLE: **£98/£125**

Tanyard

Wierton Hill, Boughton Monchelsea, Nr Maidstone, Kent ME17 4JT
Tel: 0622 744705

A small medieval country house hotel of enormous character. There are beams everywhere, a massive open fireplace with log fires in bad weather, nooks and crannies and atmospheric bedrooms of infinite olde worlde charm. In the Dining Room, owner Jan Davies presents interesting dishes on small daily changing menus. Situated in a typically English country garden complete with pond, this highly individual building should suit those who prefer the personal touch.

OPEN: **Early February to mid December**
NO. ROOMS: **6** EN SUITE **6**
ROOM TELEPHONES: **Yes** TV IN ROOMS: **Yes**
PETS: **No** CHILDREN: **Over 6**
DISABLED: **Unsuitable**

SWIMMING POOL/HEALTH CLUB: **No**
CONFERENCE FACILITIES:
No
PRICE GUIDE:
SINGLE: **£50/£60** DOUBLE: **£75/£95**

LOCATION: **Turn off B2163 opposite Cock Inn, take 1st right down Weirton Road**

Langtry Manor Hotel

Derby Road, East Cliff, Bournemouth BH1 3QB
Tel: 0202 553887 · Fax: 0202 290115

Built by King Edward VII for his mistress Lillie Langtry, this charming atmospheric hotel is a shrine to the famous couple, with memorabilia, a Son et Lumiere evoking poignant memories of this former love nest, and a host of period features. Entering the bedchambers, particularly the magnificent Edward VII Suite, one feels as though one had entered a time warp, stepping back in time, if it were not for the 20th century creature comforts. Welcome Breaks are a speciality which on Saturdays include a fabulous Edwardian Banquet served by staff dressed in Edwardian style. Langtry Manor ... an experience not to be missed.

OPEN: **All year**
NO. ROOMS: **25** EN SUITE **25**
ROOM TELEPHONES: **Yes** TV IN ROOMS: **Yes**
PETS: **By Arrangement**
CHILDREN: **By Arrangement** DISABLED: **Yes**
LOCATION: **Off Christchurch Road**

SWIMMING POOL/HEALTH CLUB: **No**
CONFERENCE FACILITIES: **Residential Small Business Meetings up to 25**
PRICE GUIDE:
SINGLE: **£59** DOUBLE: **£89/£140**

The Linthwaite House Hotel

Crook, Bowness-on-Windermere, Cumbria LA23 3JA
Tel: 05394 88600 · Fax: 05394 88601

Linthwaite House is a hotel with a difference. Beautiful interiors are warm and inviting with most imaginative colour co-ordinated furnishings and decor, rich drapes and a host of thoughtful touches. Bedrooms are quite delightful with superb bathrooms. It would be difficult to better the situation, in its own 14 acres surrounded by a magical panorama of fells and lakes. Mouth watering food is served in the romantic atmosphere of the lovely dining room. The mixture is irresistable, stunning scenery, good food and fine wines combined with supreme comfort, this is Linthwaite House.

OPEN: **All year**
NO. ROOMS: **18** EN SUITE **18**
ROOM TELEPHONES: **Yes** TV IN ROOMS: **Yes**
PETS: **No**   CHILDREN: **Over 7**
DISABLED: **Yes**
LOCATION: **Off B5284**

SWIMMING POOL/HEALTH CLUB: **Nearby**
CONFERENCE FACILITIES:
Small Business Meetings up to 18
PRICE GUIDE:
SINGLE: **£70** DOUBLE: **£100**

Farlam Hall

Brampton, Cumbria CA8 2NG
Tel: 06977 46234 · Fax: 06977 46683

One of my favourite hotels. A role model for the personally owned establishment. The Quinion and Stevenson families offer a unique combination of friendliness, comfort and superb food. Bedrooms are beautifully appointed and sure to please the most discerning guest. The ladies will love them! This mellow house is surrounded by four acres of tranquil grounds including a lake and makes an ideal base for Lakeland, the Borders and Solway Coast.

OPEN: *March to end of January*
NO. ROOMS: *13* EN SUITE *13*
ROOM TELEPHONES: *Yes* TV IN ROOMS: *Yes*
PETS: *Yes* CHILDREN: *Over 5*
DISABLED: *Unsuitable*

SWIMMING POOL/HEALTH CLUB: *No*
CONFERENCE FACILITIES: *No*
PRICE GUIDE:
SINGLE: *£95/£110 (incl Dinner)*
DOUBLE: *£160/£200 (incl Dinner)*

LOCATION: *NOT in Farlam Village – on A689 Brampton-Alston Road*

The Saunton Sands Hotel

Braunton, Devon EX33 1LQ
Tel: 0271 890212 · Fax: 0271 890145

This imposing white hotel stands in a commanding position encompassing fabulous views of miles of golden beaches washed by Atlantic rollers. Every creature comfort is catered for ... and then some more. A lift whisks you to well appointed bedrooms, many with sensational marine views. In the elegant restaurant you can enjoy good food and fine wines. There are un-rivalled leisure facilities and of course the famous championship Saunton Golf Club is adjacent. Major UK companies choose Saunton Sands for their conferences, which is hardly surprising. A stay here is a guaranteed tonic for the jaded executive.

OPEN: **All year**
NO. ROOMS: **92** EN SUITE **92**
ROOM TELEPHONES: **Yes** TV IN ROOMS: **Yes**
PETS: **No** CHILDREN: **Yes**
DISABLED: **Yes**

SWIMMING POOL: **Indoor and Outdoor**
CONFERENCE FACILITIES:
Business Meetings up to 120
PRICE GUIDE:
SINGLE: **From £61** DOUBLE: **From £120**

Chauntry House Hotel

Bray-on-Thames, Berkshire SL6 2AB
Tel: 0628 73991 · Fax: 0628 773089

Although it is a mere 15 minutes drive from Heathrow Airport, this 18th century house lies in a peaceful location twixt churchyard and village cricket pitch. Hosted by the affable Robert and Ann Young, the ambience here is relaxed and undemanding. Comfortable bedrooms have many extras, but it is as evening falls that Chauntry House takes on a particularly intimate atmosphere. In summer, aperitifs can be taken in the garden followed by really succulent food served in the charming Dining Room.

OPEN: *All year*
NO. ROOMS: *13* EN SUITE *13*
ROOM TELEPHONES: *Yes* TV IN ROOMS: *Yes*
PETS: *Yes* CHILDREN: *Yes*
DISABLED: *Yes*
LOCATION: *Off Jcn 8/9 of M4, take A308 towards Windsor and then B3028 to Bray*

SWIMMING POOL/HEALTH CLUB: *No*
CONFERENCE FACILITIES:
Small Business Meetings up to 26
PRICE GUIDE: SINGLE: *£88.15*
DOUBLE: *£105.75*

The Lygon Arms

Broadway, Worcestershire WR12 7DU
Tel: 0386 852255 · Fax: 0386 858611

One of this country's most historic hotels, The Lygon is quintessential England. From captivating period bedrooms to charming sunny rooms in the Orchard and Garden wings. Great fireplaces, blackened beams, to the Great Hall with its Minstrel's Gallery and heraldic frieze, the atmosphere of a bygone age lives on. A recent addition is a fabulous Country Club with a superb galleried Swimming Pool, Spa Bath, Sauna, Solarium, Steam Room, Fitness Studio, Beauty Salon, Terrace Restaurant and Roof Garden.

OPEN: **All year**
NO. ROOMS: **63** EN SUITE **63**
ROOM TELEPHONES: **Yes** TV IN ROOMS: **Yes**
PETS: **Yes** CHILDREN: **Yes**
DISABLED: **Yes**

SWIMMING POOL/HEALTH CLUB: **Yes**
CONFERENCE FACILITIES:
Business Meetings up to 60
PRICE GUIDE: SINGLE: **£98.70/£123.30**
DOUBLE: **£145.70/£155.10 (inc Cont Bkfst)**

Dormy House Hotel

Willersey Hill, Broadway, Worcestershire WR12 7LF
Tel: 0386 852711 · Fax: 0386 858636

This unusual and attractive hotel, once a 17th century farmhouse, sits in a commanding position overlooking the verdant Vale of Evesham. An interesting arrangement of rooms opening off one another, with beams, log fires, various nooks and crannies and imaginative use of exposed stone add to the immense charm of this delightful hotel. Strikingly designed bedrooms are highly distinctive with excellent bathrooms. Businessmen are especially well catered for ... tourists will love it!

OPEN: **All year except Christmas**
NO. ROOMS: **49** EN SUITE **49**
ROOM TELEPHONES: **Yes** TV IN ROOMS: **Yes**
PETS: **Yes** CHILDREN: **Yes**
DISABLED: **Yes**

SWIMMING POOL/HEALTH CLUB: **No**
CONFERENCE FACILITIES:
Theatre Style up to 180
PRICE GUIDE:
SINGLE: **£50/£55** DOUBLE: **£100/£110**

LOCATION: **Half mile off A44 halfway up Broadway Hill**

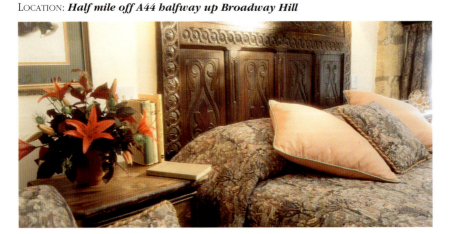

Careys Manor Hotel

Brockenhurst, New Forest, Hampshire SO42 7RH
Tel: 0590 23551 · Fax: 0590 22799

This former Royal Hunting Lodge, whose origins date back to the days of King Charles 2nd, has in the Carat Club what is undoubtedly the finest Health Complex in the New Forest. Facilities include a superb Gymnasium with full time physiotherapist, a magnificent ozone Swimming Pool with Jet Stream, Jacuzzi, Sauna, Solarium, Steam Room and Beauty Therapist. Bedrooms, some with 4-posters and balconies, are very comfortable with excellent bathrooms and food is interesting and varied. In the heart of the Forest, there's something for everyone at Careys Manor.

OPEN: **All year**
NO. ROOMS: **79** EN SUITE **79**
ROOM TELEPHONES: **Yes** TV IN ROOMS: **Yes**
PETS: **Yes** CHILDREN: **Yes**
DISABLED: **Yes**

SWIMMING POOL/HEALTH CLUB: **Yes**
CONFERENCE FACILITIES:
Up to 40 Residential Delegates
PRICE GUIDE:
SINGLE: **£77.90** DOUBLE: **£99.90**

Needwood Manor Hotel
Rangemore, Burton-on-Trent
Tel: 0283 712932

Two acres of lovely grounds surround this 19th century Manor operated by friendly owners, Mr & Mrs George. The house is full of character and has splendidly proportioned public rooms and comfortable bedrooms. The atmosphere here is relaxed and informal with log fires in winter and fresh flowers in summer. Good food is served in the attractive dining room and noteworthy architectural features include the fascinating Pitch Pine staircase and Gallery.

OPEN: **All year**
NO. ROOMS: **9** EN SUITE **5**
ROOM TELEPHONES: **Yes** TV IN ROOMS: **Yes**
PETS: **No** CHILDREN: **Yes**
DISABLED: **Yes**

SWIMMING POOL/HEALTH CLUB: **No**
CONFERENCE FACILITIES:
Small Business Meetings up to 20
PRICE GUIDE:
SINGLE: **£56/£66** DOUBLE: **£69/£84**

The Angel Hotel

Bury St. Edmunds, Suffolk IP33 1LT
Tel: 0284 753926 · Fax: 0284 750092

Dating from 1452, this creeper clad building overlooks the ancient Norman Abbey of St. Edmund with its colourful gardens. The Angel is relaxed and comfortable with its easy chairs, fresh flowers and log fires in winter. Individually furnished bedrooms have all 20th century facilities. For eating you can choose from the main Dining Room with its classic and traditional English dishes, including roasts, or in the Vaults sample more simple fare in informal, though medieval, surroundings. Charles Dickens featured The Angel and Bedroom 15 in Mr Pickwick.

OPEN: **All year**
NO. ROOMS: **40** EN SUITE **40**
ROOM TELEPHONES: **Yes** TV IN ROOMS: **Yes**
PETS: **Yes** CHILDREN: **Yes**
DISABLED: **By arrangement**

SWIMMING POOL/HEALTH CLUB: **No**
CONFERENCE FACILITIES:
Business Meetings up to 140
PRICE GUIDE: SINGLE: **£69**
DOUBLE: **£99/£125**

Howfield Manor

Chartham Hatch, Canterbury, Kent CT4 7HQ
Tel: 0227 738294 · Fax: 0227 731535

An extensive programme of upgrading by the Towns family has transformed this old Manor House, whilst successfully retaining the original period character. Bedrooms are delightful, tastefully designed and well appointed with excellent bathrooms. Unique features are the illuminated old Well in the Restaurant floor, a priesthole in the Bar and trompe d'oeil murals. Appetising food, oak beams and log fires add to the ambience.

OPEN: *All year*
NO. ROOMS: *13* EN SUITE *13*
ROOM TELEPHONES: *Yes* TV IN ROOMS: *Yes*
PETS: *No* CHILDREN: *Over 10*
DISABLED: *Unsuitable*

SWIMMING POOL/HEALTH CLUB: *No*
CONFERENCE FACILITIES:
Business meetings up to 50
PRICE GUIDE:
SINGLE: *£60* DOUBLE: *£80/£90*

LOCATION: *Off A28 Ashford – Canterbury road 2 miles out of Canterbury towards Ashford*

The Nare Hotel

Carne Beach, Veryan-in-Roseland, Truro, S Cornwall TR2 5PF
Tel: 0872 501279 · Fax: 0872 501856

It is rare to find the comfort and relaxed atmosphere of a quality country house combined with a spectacular coastal location. In the case of the Nare, you have both. Antiques, log fires and fresh flowers grace public rooms. Bedrooms, many with their own sea facing balconies, are furnished with taste, de luxe rooms being particularly spacious. The elegant dining room with its graceful arched windows commands panoramic views of Gerrans Bay and offers and excellent choice of good English fare with many local Cornish specialities. As an escape from the hurly burly of 20th century life, it would be difficult to better the Nare.

OPEN: **All year**
NO. ROOMS: **38** EN SUITE **38**
ROOM TELEPHONES: **Yes** TV IN ROOMS: **Yes**
PETS: **Yes**   CHILDREN: **Yes**
DISABLED: **Yes**

SWIMMING POOL: **Outdoor Heated**
CONFERENCE FACILITIES:
Small Business Meetings up to 30
PRICE GUIDE:
SINGLE: **£41/£93** DOUBLE: **£82/£156**

Aynsome Manor

Cartmel, Nr Grange-over-Sands, Cumbria LA11 6HH
Tel: 05395 36653

In the timeless Vale of Cartmel near the Priory stands this charming old Manor House which is owned and loved by the friendly Varley family. In the elegant candle-lit atmosphere of the Dining Room, graced by a superb original oil painting, you will enjoy delicious home cooking utilising fresh (not frozen) food. Bedrooms are cosy as is the small bar and you can relax in one of two lounges with their serene views of the countryside and open fires in winter. Ideally located for touring Lakeland and the Lancashire coast.

OPEN: *February to December inclusive*
NO. ROOMS: *13* EN SUITE *12*
ROOM TELEPHONES: *Yes* TV IN ROOMS: *Yes*
PETS: *Yes* CHILDREN: *Yes*
DISABLED: *Unsuitable*
LOCATION: *Off A590 signposted Cartmel*

SWIMMING POOL/HEALTH CLUB: *No*
CONFERENCE FACILITIES: *No*
PRICE GUIDE:
SINGLE: *£52*
DOUBLE: *£104 (incl Dinner)*

Brockencote Hall

Chaddesley Corbett, Nr Kidderminster, Worcestershire DY10 4PY
Tel: 0562 777876 · Fax: 0562 777872

This gracious and imposing building sits in 70 acres of glorious grounds including a placid lake and fine specimen trees. Owners Joseph and Alison Petitjean have established a considerable reputation for their innovative French and English dishes presented with great finesse in the elegant surroundings of their lovely Restaurant with its cool, classic decor. All the charming bedrooms have superb views and have been furnished and designed in sympathy with the period style of the house.

OPEN: **All year**
NO. ROOMS: **8** EN SUITE **8**
ROOM TELEPHONES: **Yes** TV IN ROOMS: **Yes**
PETS: **No** CHILDREN: **Yes**
DISABLED: **Unsuitable**

SWIMMING POOL/HEALTH CLUB: **No**
CONFERENCE FACILITIES:
Small Business Meetings up to 15
PRICE GUIDE:
SINGLE: **£62** DOUBLE: **£90**

LOCATION: **Off A448 five miles from Bromsgrove, three miles Kidderminster**

The Manor

Chadlington, Oxfordshire OX7 3LL
Tel: 0608 76711

Owners David and Chris Grant set out to provide their guests with a memorable experience, i.e. to give them the flavour of a genuine country house. You are made to feel more like house guests. The ambience is relaxed and friendly. The entire Manor is beautifully furnished with superb drapes and with most appealing bedrooms, and is run in a personal and highly individual fashion by the owners. Chris Grant is responsible for the appetising and artistically presented food whilst David looks after the Restaurant and wines.

OPEN: *All year*
NO. ROOMS: 7 EN SUITE 7
ROOM TELEPHONES: *Yes* TV IN ROOMS: *Yes*
PETS: *No* CHILDREN: *Yes*
DISABLED: *Unsuitable*
LOCATION: *Three miles south east of Chipping Norton*

SWIMMING POOL/HEALTH CLUB: *No*
CONFERENCE FACILITIES:
Small Business Meetings up to 7
PRICE GUIDE:
SINGLE: *£65/£80* DOUBLE: *£100/£120*

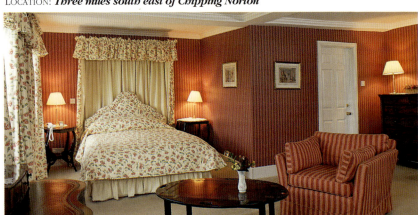

Great Tree Hotel

Sandy Park, Nr Chagford, Devon TQ13 8JS
Tel: 0647 432491

This is a hotel with a very nice "feel" to it. Sometimes it is hard to define but perhaps it is because of the welcome accorded by owners Mr & Mrs Eaton Gray. There are some interesting features to this Colonial style former hunting lodge, like the beautiful carved wood staircase and vaulted ceiling in the charming Lounge. Bedrooms are cosy and comfortable and overlook the gardens. In the pleasant Dining Room fresh produce from the hotel's own garden forms the basis of daily changing menus. Peacefully located in its own 18 acres with superb views of Dartmoor, Great Tree represents good value for money.

OPEN: **All year**
NO. ROOMS: **12** EN SUITE **12**
ROOM TELEPHONES: **Yes** TV IN ROOMS: **Yes**
PETS: **Yes**   CHILDREN: **Yes**
DISABLED: **Unsuitable**
LOCATION: **Two miles south of A30 off A382**

SWIMMING POOL/HEALTH CLUB: **No**
CONFERENCE FACILITIES:
Business Meetings by arrangement
PRICE GUIDE: SINGLE: **£48/£60**
DOUBLE: **£75/£95**

On The Park

Evesham Road, Cheltenham, Gloucestershire GL52 2AH
Tel: 0242 518898 · Fax: 0242 511526

This elegant Town House overlooking a peaceful park, is a classic example of a Regency villa. Beautifully restored and furnished in highly individual style, the hotel offers sophisticated standards of civilised creature comforts for the discerning guest. Note the hand stencilling in bedrooms and superb grapevine cornicing in the Epicurean Restaurant where the finest in modern British cooking can be sampled, presented by chef Patrick McDonald. Although a town house, On The Park has all the authentic atmosphere of a fine Country House Hotel.

OPEN: *All year*
NO. ROOMS: *8* EN SUITE *8*
ROOM TELEPHONES: *Yes* TV IN ROOMS: *Yes*
PETS: *No* CHILDREN: *Over 8*
DISABLED: *Unsuitable*
LOCATION: *On main Evesham Road*

SWIMMING POOL/HEALTH CLUB: *No*
CONFERENCE FACILITIES:
Small Business Meetings
PRICE GUIDE:
SINGLE: *£74.50* DOUBLE: *£89*

St David's Park Hotel

St David's Park, Ewloe, Clwyd CH5 3YB
Tel: 0244 520800 · Fax: 0244 520930

The impact is immediate as soon as you glimpse this stunning modern hotel built to the highest standards in elegant Georgian style. Interiors are quite lovely, all public rooms being air-conditioned and richly furnished. Splendid bedrooms are well appointed with luxury bathrooms. In the Fountains Restaurant there is a choice of a la carte or buffet style cuisine. With its 3 boardrooms and 6 syndicate rooms, this hotel is perfect for conferences. Top all this with a superb Leisure Club and you have a mixture that adds up to one of the finest hotels in the North.

OPEN: *All year*
NO. ROOMS: *121* EN SUITE *121*
ROOM TELEPHONES: *Yes* TV IN ROOMS: *Yes*
PETS: *No* CHILDREN: *Yes*
DISABLED: *Yes*
LOCATION: *At jcn of A55/A494 head for Queensferry A494 & then left on B5127 signed Buckley*

SWIMMING POOL/HEALTH CLUB: *Yes*
CONFERENCE FACILITIES:
Business Meetings up to 200
PRICE GUIDE:
SINGLE: *£72* DOUBLE: *£83 (Room Only)*

Nunsmere Hall

Tarporley Road, Sandiway, Cheshire CW8 2ES
Tel: 0606 889100 · Fax: 0606 889055

It would be difficult to imagine a setting more enchanting than that enjoyed by this elegant hotel, which lies on its own wooded peninsula surrounded on three sides by a tranquil lake. This is all the more extraordinary when one considers that the M6 Motorway is so easily accessible. A major refurbishment programme has turned Nunsmere Hall into what is arguably Cheshire's finest privately owned hotel. Interiors are full of interest, bedrooms being extremely comfortable with unusual decor, the latest ones being particularly spacious and superbly equipped with magnificent bathrooms.

OPEN: **All year**
NO. ROOMS: **32** EN SUITE **32**
ROOM TELEPHONES: **Yes** TV IN ROOMS: **Yes**
PETS: **No** CHILDREN: **Yes**
DISABLED: **Yes**
LOCATION: **Off A49 ten miles from Chester**

SWIMMING POOL/HEALTH CLUB: **No**
CONFERENCE FACILITIES:
Small Business Meetings up to 35
PRICE GUIDE:
SINGLE: **£95** DOUBLE: **£120/£200**

The Ship Hotel

North Street, Chichester, West Sussex PO19 1NH
Tel: 0243 782028 · Fax: 0243 774254

This one time Admiral's home is now Chichester's finest hotel. Elegant interiors enhanced with pillars, are beautifully furnished and appointed. A graceful staircase leads to delightful bedrooms. The Ship's marine background is reflected in prints and paintings of ships and naval battles, barometers and brass cannons, not to mention the aptly named bedrooms which echo England's history. In the charming Restaurant you can dine on French/English cuisine before retiring to a comfortable bed.

OPEN: **All year**
NO. ROOMS: **37** EN SUITE **37**
ROOM TELEPHONES: **Yes** TV IN ROOMS: **Yes**
PETS: **Yes** CHILDREN: **Yes**
DISABLED: **Unsuitable**

SWIMMING POOL/HEALTH CLUB: **No**
CONFERENCE FACILITIES:
Small Business Meetings up to 40
PRICE GUIDE:
SINGLE: **£40/£63** DOUBLE: **£60/£92**

The Cotswold House Hotel

Chipping Campden, Gloucestershire GL55 6AN
Tel: 0386 840330 · Fax: 0386 840310

Pass through the pillar flanked front door and you enter an elegant Entrance Hall with more pillars and a graceful spiral staircase which leads to luxurious bedrooms, each with its own theme. Fine antiques adorn the public rooms and in the beautifully proportioned Dining Room, which overlooks the garden, interesting dishes are presented. Owned and operated by Robert and Gill Greenstock, this charming 17th century Cotswold house is a delight for those seeking something a little bit special.

OPEN: *All year*
NO. ROOMS: *15* EN SUITE *15*
ROOM TELEPHONES: *Yes* TV IN ROOMS: *Yes*
PETS: *No* CHILDREN: *Over 8*
DISABLED: *Unsuitable*

SWIMMING POOL/HEALTH CLUB: *No*
CONFERENCE FACILITIES:
Small Business Meetings (Winter) up to 15
PRICE GUIDE:
SINGLE: *£60/£75* DOUBLE: *£90/£126*

The Redfern Hotel

Cleobury Mortimer, Shropshire DY14 8AA
Tel: 0299 270395 · Fax: 0299 271011

"A warm welcome in the heart of England" is the slogan on the hotel's brochure, and that is what you get from owners Jon and Liz Redfern. Real ale, log fires, comfortable bedrooms and good "home cooking", this is The Redfern. The English Kitchen Restaurant is what its name suggests, it certainly is an unusual setting for dining. Home cured hams and bacon hang from the beams! Breakfast if served in an elevated Conservatory as are snacks and a buffet. Echoes of its Norman past linger in the charmingly named Cleobury Mortimer, at the centre of which is The Redfern.

OPEN: **All year**
NO. ROOMS: **11** EN SUITE **11**
ROOM TELEPHONES: **Yes** TV IN ROOMS: **Yes**
PETS: **Yes** CHILDREN: **Yes**
DISABLED: **Unsuitable**
LOCATION: **On B4117 out of Ludlow**

SWIMMING POOL/HEALTH CLUB: **No**
CONFERENCE FACILITIES:
Small Business Meetings up to 20
PRICE GUIDE:
SINGLE: **£48** DOUBLE: **From £68**

The White Hart Hotel

Market End, Coggeshall, Essex CO6 1H
Tel: 0376 561654 · Fax: 0376 561789

This incredibly picturesque hotel dating back to the 13th century retains all the character and atmosphere of a bygone age. There is a magnificent lounge with beamed vaulted ceiling, exposed stone walls and a great open fireplace. Cosy bedrooms are tastefully furnished in keeping with the period. Food is noteworthy here, great importance being placed on the choice of ingredients to form the basis of the delicious food, with emphasis on Italian specialities.

OPEN: *All year*
NO. ROOMS: *18* EN SUITE *18*
ROOM TELEPHONES: *Yes* TV IN ROOMS: *Yes*
PETS: *No* CHILDREN: *By arrangement*
DISABLED: *Unsuitable*

SWIMMING POOL/HEALTH CLUB: *No*
CONFERENCE FACILITIES:
Up to 24 Boardroom 35 Theatre Style
PRICE GUIDE:
SINGLE: *£61.50/£67* DOUBLE: *£82/£97*

LOCATION: *Off the A12 take signs for Kelvedon & then the B1024 to Coggeshall*

Coulsworthy House

Combe Martin, N. Devon EX34 0PD
Tel: 0271 882463

The Anthony's and the Osmonds own and operate this pleasant family hotel, noted for the excellence of Alison Osmonds original cooking skills. She utilises fresh local produce as the basis for her appetising dishes. The atmosphere is that of a home with a relaxed good humoured air, nothing pretentious here. The views from the garden down the Combe to the sea beyond are quite magnificent. Bedrooms are pleasing but you won't find telephones or tea-makers with that awful UHT milk. Old fashioned standards of service live on at Coulsworthy.

OPEN: **February 8th to December 7th**
NO. ROOMS: **9** EN SUITE **9**
ROOM TELEPHONES: **No** TV IN ROOMS: **Yes**
PETS: **No** CHILDREN: **Yes**
DISABLED: **Unsuitable**
LOCATION: **Off A399 halfway between Blackmoor Gate and Combe Martin**

SWIMMING POOL: **Outdoor Heated**
CONFERENCE FACILITIES: **No**
PRICE GUIDE:
SINGLE: **£55/£120 (incl Dinner)**
DOUBLE: **£108/£160 (incl Dinner)**

Treglos Hotel

Constantine Bay, Nr Padstow, Cornwall PL28 8JH
Tel: 0841 520727 · Fax: 0841 521163

Within 40 minutes of 10 golf courses, with special golf inclusive tariff, situated on the bracing North Cornish coast in sight of Atlantic rollers, this delightful Country House Hotel is perhaps the finest on this coast. There are five appealing lounges, a pleasant bar and in the lovely beamed Restaurant you can choose from a 6 course table d'hote menu or the more extensive a la carte. Opening on to the garden is the superb Swimming Pool and Jacuzzi. Bedrooms are extremely comfortable, most have sea views, some their own balconies. Traditional standards of service live on at Treglos which for over 30 years has been owned by Mr and Mrs Ted Barlow, now joined by Mr and Mrs Jim Barlow.

OPEN: ***Early March to early November***
NO. ROOMS: **44** EN SUITE **44**
ROOM TELEPHONES: **Yes** TV IN ROOMS: **Yes**
PETS: **Yes** CHILDREN: **Yes**
DISABLED: **Yes**

SWIMMING POOL: **Yes**
CONFERENCE FACILITIES: **No**
PRICE GUIDE:
SINGLE: ***£50/£68 (incl Dinner)***
DOUBLE: ***£100/£145 (incl Dinner)***
LOCATION: ***Turn off B3276 Coast Road through St. Merryn & right for Constantine Bay***

The Old Cloth Hall

Cranbrook, Kent TN17 3NR
Tel: 0580 712220

This dream house stands in beautiful gardens, the magnificent 12 acres of grounds contain many rare shrubs and trees, the rhododendrons and azaleas a blaze of colour. I'm sure Queen Elizabeth 1st, who was once a visitor, would very much approve if she could return today. Owned and operated in a very personal way by Katherine Morgan, this house is a delight and its massive inglenook fireplace, oak panelling, chintzy furnishings and fresh flowers. Lovely bedrooms one with a fabulous 4-poster, are in keeping with the house and finest home-cooking is based on fresh garden produce.

OPEN: ***All year***
NO. ROOMS: ***3*** EN SUITE ***3***
ROOM TELEPHONES: ***Yes*** TV IN ROOMS: ***Yes***
PETS: ***No*** CHILDREN: ***Yes***
DISABLED: ***Unsuitable***
LOCATION: ***One mile from Cranbrook on Golford Road towards Tenterden***

SWIMMING POOL: ***Outdoor***
CONFERENCE FACILITIES: ***No***
PRICE GUIDE:
SINGLE: ***£45/£50*** DOUBLE: ***£95***

Cricklade Hotel

Common Hill, Cricklade, Wiltshire SN6 6HA
Tel: 0793 750751 · Fax: 0793 751767

A great deal of thought has gone into the extensive upgrading of this fine hotel, interior designs are tasteful with extremely comfortable furnishings. The bedrooms are very well appointed with many extras and food of rare quality is served in the attractive Dining Room. Impressive though this is, the big plus point for Cricklade is its superb Country Club with its un-rivalled range of facilities, own Golf Course, Tennis, Snooker, Pool, Spa Bath, Steam Room, Solarium and Gymnasium.

OPEN: **All year**
NO. ROOMS: **44** EN SUITE **44**
ROOM TELEPHONES: **Yes** TV IN ROOMS: **Yes**
PETS: **No** CHILDREN: **No**
DISABLED: **Yes**
LOCATION: **Off B4040 Malmesbury – Cricklade road**

SWIMMING POOL/HEALTH CLUB:
Yes, Indoor Heated
CONFERENCE FACILITIES: **Up to 120**
PRICE GUIDE: SINGLE: **£74/£78**
DOUBLE: **£86/£90**

Fingals

Old Coombe, Dittisham, Dartmouth, Devon TQ5 0JA
Tel: 080422 398 · Fax: 080422 401

Described by owner Richard Johnston as a "get-away-from-the-routine-hotel-hotel" this is no exaggeration. Fingals is definitely relaxed and informal. You are not expected to dress for dinner. The highly personal way Fingals is operated reflects the philosophy of its charismatic owner. The location is tranquil, the gardens well manicured, the peace is absolute. Much use has been made of natural wood in the decor which gives interiors their mellow warmth. Fresh local produce forms the basis for the succulent 4 course dinners. With its wide ranging leisure facilities Fingals is ideal for those seeking "something different".

OPEN: **Easter to end Dec**
NO. ROOMS: **9** EN SUITE **9**
ROOM TELEPHONES: **Yes**
TV IN ROOMS: **By arrangement**
PETS: **Yes** CHILDREN: **Yes**
DISABLED: **Unsuitable**

SWIMMING POOL: **Yes**
CONFERENCE FACILITIES:
Small Business Meetings for 15-20
PRICE GUIDE:
SINGLE: **£55** DOUBLE: **£75**

The Izaak Walton Hotel

Dovedale, Nr Ashbourne, Derbyshire DE6 2AY
Tel: 033529 555 · Fax: 033529 539

Extensive re-furbishment in 1991 has resulted in a most comfortable hotel. Named after the author of the famous "Compleat Angler", the hotel is owned by the Duke of Rutland whose oil paintings from Belvoir Castle and Haddon Hall add to the ambience. Bedrooms are well equipped with every convenience whilst public rooms have log fires and tasteful furnishings. An extensive selection of interesting dishes are featured in the Dining Room with its lovely views of the rugged Peak District scenery.

OPEN: ***All year***
NO. ROOMS: ***34*** EN SUITE ***34***
ROOM TELEPHONES: ***Yes*** TV IN ROOMS: ***Yes***
PETS: ***Yes*** CHILDREN: ***Yes***
DISABLED: ***Yes***
LOCATION: ***Off A515 through Thorpe Village***

SWIMMING POOL/HEALTH CLUB: ***No***
CONFERENCE FACILITIES:
Small Business Meetings up to 30
PRICE GUIDE:
SINGLE: ***£70*** DOUBLE: ***£90***

The Carnarvon Arms Hotel

Dulverton, Somerset
Tel: 0398 23302 · Fax: 0398 24022

Owned and operated since 1958 by Mrs Toni Jones, it is perhaps the relaxed atmosphere combined with old fashioned standards of courtesy as well as the quality of the privately owned salmon and trout waters that brings back regulars again and again. An unusual feature are the old railway buildings dating from the last century. With its cosy public rooms, open fires, gleaming copper and brass, comfortable bedrooms and good honest English cooking, the Carnarvon Arms typifies all that is best in the English Country House Hotel.

OPEN: **Closed three weeks February**
NO. ROOMS: **25** EN SUITE **23**
ROOM TELEPHONES: **Yes** TV IN ROOMS: **Yes**
PETS: **Yes** CHILDREN: **Yes**
DISABLED: **Yes**
LOCATION: **Just off B3222 south of Dulverton**

SWIMMING POOL: **Outside Heated**
CONFERENCE FACILITIES:
Up to 100 theatre style
PRICE GUIDE:
SINGLE: **£37/£47** DOUBLE: **£64/£94**

The Evesham Hotel

Coopers Lane, off Waterside, Evesham, Worcestershire WR11 6DA
Tel: 0386 765566 · Fax: 0386 765443

A rich vein of humour pervades this comfortable hotel, the main part of which dates from 1540, and which is owned and operated by the friendly Jenkinson family. Look out for Teddy Bears on your door keys and Rubber Ducks in the bath! Good food is served in the elegant Georgian Room overlooking a magnificent 180 year old Cedar of Lebanon. There is a fabulous wine list and unique range of liqueurs. The Evesham is ideally placed for touring the historic Cotswolds and Shakespeare country.

OPEN: **All year**
NO. ROOMS: **40** EN SUITE **40**
ROOM TELEPHONES: **Yes** TV IN ROOMS: **Yes**
PETS: **Yes** CHILDREN: **Yes**
DISABLED: **Unsuitable**
LOCATION: **Up from the River Avon**

SWIMMING POOL: **Yes**
Indoor Heated
CONFERENCE FACILITIES:
Small Business Meetings
PRICE GUIDE: SINGLE: **£64** DOUBLE: **£90**

The Royal Duchy Hotel

Cliff Road, Falmouth, S Cornwall TR17 4NX
Tel: 0326 313042 · Fax: 0326 319420

Situated on the sea front of this historic maritime town a mere stone's throw from Falmouth Bay, lies The Royal Duchy. Total re-furbishment has turned this into one of the finest hotels in the area. Cuisine of high standard is backed by 24 hour room service. Bedrooms, most overlooking the Bay are models of comfort and are served by a lift to all floors. With its excellent swimming pool and leisure complex, the Royal Duchy makes an excellent base for touring the Cornish Riviera.

OPEN: **All year**
NO. ROOMS: **50** EN SUITE **50**
ROOM TELEPHONES: **Yes** TV IN ROOMS: **Yes**
PETS: **No** CHILDREN: **Yes**
DISABLED: **Yes**

SWIMMING POOL: **Indoor**
CONFERENCE FACILITIES:
Business Meetings up to 60
PRICE GUIDE:
SINGLE: **From £47** DOUBLE: **From £81**

Hotel St Michaels

Gyllyngvase Beach, Falmouth, S Cornwall TR11 4NB
Tel: 0326 312707 · Fax: 0326 211772

This long low hotel set in its own award winning gardens overlooks the beach and sparkling blue waters of Falmouth Bay. It offers something for all tastes, from holidays for all the family to full conference facilities for the businessman. Bedrooms are comfortable and well appointed. The air conditioned restaurant offers a comprehensive choice from table d'hote and a la carte menus whilst the impressive Health Complex includes a fine pool, trimnasium, sauna, jacuzzis and hair salon.

OPEN: **All year**
NO. ROOMS: **70** EN SUITE **70**
ROOM TELEPHONES: **Yes** TV IN ROOMS: **Yes**
PETS: **Yes** CHILDREN: **Yes**
DISABLED: **Yes**

SWIMMING POOL/HEALTH CLUB: **Yes**
CONFERENCE FACILITIES:
Business Meetings up to 200
PRICE GUIDE:
SINGLE: **£43/£61** DOUBLE: **£90/£110**

Meudon

Mawnan Smith, Nr Falmouth, S Cornwall TR11 5HT
Tel: 0326 250541 · Fax: 0326 250543

Surrounded by National Trust land, this mellow old Cornish house is situated in stunning sub-tropical gardens leading to the sea and its own private beach. The lovely hanging gardens are the work of renowned garden designer "Capability" Brown and the grounds abound with many rare and exotic shrubs and trees. You can enjoy this visual feast from the delightful restaurant at the same time as feasting on the superb traditional English fare which includes many Cornish specialities. Meudon is privately owned by Mr Harry Pilgrim.

OPEN: **February to December**
NO. ROOMS: **32** EN SUITE **32**
ROOM TELEPHONES: **Yes** TV IN ROOMS: **Yes**
PETS: **Yes** CHILDREN: **By arrangement**
DISABLED: **By arrangement**

SWIMMING POOL/HEALTH CLUB: **No**
CONFERENCE FACILITIES:
No
PRICE GUIDE: SINGLE: **£66.50/£90**
DOUBLE: **£120/£160 (inc Dinner)**

Stock Hill Country House Hotel

Gillingham, Dorset SP8 5NR
Tel: 0747 823626 · Fax: 0747 825628

This lovely country house hotel is the creation of Austrian Peter Hauser and his wife Nita. Deep in the heart of Thomas Hardy country this is an oasis of good living in an area not particularly blessed with worthwhile hotels. Peter is the chef and produces imaginative and delicious dishes based on fresh local ingredients, not surprisingly perhaps, great emphasis being placed on mouth watering deserts. Supremely comfortable throughout, the furnishings have been chosen with great care and feature many fine antiques.

OPEN: **All year**
NO. ROOMS: **9** EN SUITE **9**
ROOM TELEPHONES: **Yes** TV IN ROOMS: **Yes**
PETS: **No** CHILDREN: **Over 8**
DISABLED: **Unsuitable**
LOCATION: **On the B3081**

SWIMMING POOL/HEALTH CLUB: **No**
CONFERENCE FACILITIES: **No**
PRICE GUIDE:
SINGLE: **£75/£110** DOUBLE: **£150/£220**
(inc Dinner)

The Old Rectory

Great Snoring, Fakenham, Norfolk NR21 0HP
Tel: 0328 820597 · Fax: 0328 820048

No matter how jaded you may feel after your journey, the peace and tranquillity that pervades this former Manor House will quickly work its magic on you. Of unusual architectural interest with its mullioned windows and terra cotta tiles, the Rectory stands in a lovely walled garden. Truly England as it used to be. Comfortable bedrooms are furnished in traditional style, public rooms are restful, food is good home cooking. Tea can be taken on the lawn in summer. For those seeking total privacy enquire about the superb Cottage Suites.

OPEN: ***All year***
NO. ROOMS: **6** EN SUITE **6**
ROOM TELEPHONES: ***Yes*** TV IN ROOMS: ***Yes***
PETS: ***No*** CHILDREN: ***Over 12***
DISABLED: ***Unsuitable***
LOCATION: ***Signed off A148 Fakenham – Cromer road***

SWIMMING POOL/HEALTH CLUB: ***No***
CONFERENCE FACILITIES: ***No***
PRICE GUIDE:
SINGLE: ***£65*** DOUBLE: ***£85***

Horn of Plenty

Gulworthy, Tavistock, Devon PL19 8JD
Tel: 0822 832528 · Fax: 0822 832528

Looking across the verdant valley in late summer, the scene is reminiscent of a Samuel Palmer landscape. As its name suggests, this charming hotel takes food very seriously and utilises fresh produce for the interesting and creative dishes which appear on the menus. Bedrooms are comfortable, those in the Coach House having their own balconies and all enjoy that fabulous view of valley and moorland. Owned and operated in an informal and relaxed way by Elaine and Ian Gatehouse, the ambience is one of warmth and welcome with comfy chairs, fresh flowers in summer, log fires in winter.

OPEN: **All year**
NO. ROOMS: 7 EN SUITE 7
ROOM TELEPHONES: **Yes** TV IN ROOMS: **Yes**
PETS: **Yes** CHILDREN: **Over 13**
DISABLED: **Yes**
LOCATION: **From Tavistock take A390 and in 3 miles turn right at Gulworthy X**

SWIMMING POOL/HEALTH CLUB: **No**
CONFERENCE FACILITIES:
Small Business Meetings up to 12
PRICE GUIDE:
SINGLE: **£57/£65** DOUBLE: **£80/£88**

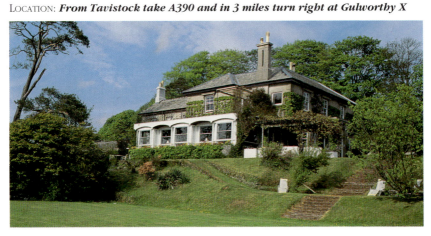

Maryland Health Hydro & Country Hotel

Harbertonford, Nr Totnes, Devon TQ9 7PT
Tel: 0803 732850 · Fax: 0803 732038

This unusual and luxurious small Health Hydro is the brain child of Theresa Barrett and is sure to make an impact. Opened August 1992 it sets out to pamper, not starve you. Just a few of the facilities are, indoor and outdoor pools, toning suite, beauty salon, hairdressing, solarium, fitness suite, tennis, steam room and croquet. Bedrooms are fresh and appealing with good bathrooms. There is a cosy bar and truly delightful restaurant serving delicious food. Fully trained staff are on hand at all times. Maryland lies twixt the sea and moors in beautiful Devon.

OPEN: **All year**
NO. ROOMS: **6** EN SUITE **6**
ROOM TELEPHONES: **Yes** TV IN ROOMS: **Yes**
PETS: **No** CHILDREN: **Over 16**
DISABLED: **Unsuitable**

SWIMMING POOL/HEALTH CLUB: **Yes**
CONFERENCE FACILITIES: **Enquire**
PRICE GUIDE: SINGLE: **£95** DOUBLE: **£160**
(inc Full Board/Complimentary Treatments/Facilities)

LOCATION: **Off A381 Totnes - Harbertonford Rd turn left just before Harbertonford**

Nidd Hall

Nidd, Harrogate, N. Yorks HG3 3BN
Tel: 0423 771598 · Fax: 0423 770931

This impressive listed Georgian style building is situated on its own 45 acres of grounds and is of considerable architectural interest. Public rooms are very much in the grand manner, with elaborate plasterwork and wrought iron much in evidence. Each of the bedrooms has been individually designed with tasteful colour schemes and enjoy views of the grounds. Notable for the excellence of its cuisine, the kitchen is under the direction of a top international chef who is responsible for creative and original dishes. Nidd Hall also offers its guests extensive Leisure facilities.

OPEN: **All year**
NO. ROOMS: **59** EN SUITE **59**
ROOM TELEPHONES: **Yes** TV IN ROOMS: **Yes**
PETS: **No** CHILDREN: **Yes**
DISABLED: **Yes**
LOCATION: **Five miles north of Harrogate just off A61**

SWIMMING POOL/HEALTH CLUB: **Yes**
CONFERENCE FACILITIES:
Business Meetings up to 120
PRICE GUIDE:
SINGLE: **£75/£90** DOUBLE: **£120/£165**

Studley Hotel

Swan Road, Harrogate, Yorks HG1 2SE
Tel: 0423 560425 · Fax: 0423 530967

This attractive hotel is situated near the lovely Valley Gardens within a stroll of the city centre and all conference venues. The pretty bedrooms have many extras and excellent bathrooms. Choose from Au Charbon de Bois French Restaurant or Shrimps Sea Food Restaurant, which as its name suggests specialises in fresh seafood. For business or pleasure the Studley makes an ideal base for this most gracious of cities.

OPEN: **All year**
NO. ROOMS: **36** EN SUITE **36**
ROOM TELEPHONES: **Yes** TV IN ROOMS: **Yes**
PETS: **By arrangement** CHILDREN: **Over 8**
DISABLED: **Unsuitable**

SWIMMING POOL/HEALTH CLUB: **No**
CONFERENCE FACILITIES:
Small Business Meetings up to 15
PRICE GUIDE:
SINGLE: **£69.50** DOUBLE: **£85**

Hob Green

Markington, Harrogate, N. Yorkshire HG3 3PJ
Tel: 0423 770031 · Fax: 0423 771589

This enchanting small hotel is situated in its own delightful award winning gardens. Antiques, log fires and original oil paintings grace the pleasingly proportioned public rooms. Each bedroom is furnished and equipped to high standards with many delightful extras, i.e. refrigerators and electric blankets. In the elegant Dining Room truly excellent food is served, much of the produce coming from the hotel's own kitchen garden.

OPEN: **All year**
NO. ROOMS: **12** EN SUITE **12**
ROOM TELEPHONES: **Yes** TV IN ROOMS: **Yes**
PETS: **Yes** CHILDREN: **Yes**
DISABLED: **Unsuitable**
LOCATION: **Turn off A61 Harrogate – Ripon road**

SWIMMING POOL/HEALTH CLUB: **No**
CONFERENCE FACILITIES:
Small Business Meetings up to 10
PRICE GUIDE: SINGLE: **£65**
DOUBLE: **£78/85** SUITE: **£105**

Farthings
Hatch Beauchamp, Somerset TA3 6SG
Tel: 0823 480664

Since the advent of the by-pass, this charming Georgian Country House Hotel now lies in a pastoral backwater, easy to get to, but nestling in rural tranquillity. Privately owned and run in a very personal and friendly fashion, Farthings offers high standards of accommodation in individually designed bedrooms. There is a small a la carte menu featuring tempting dishes based on English and French cuisine. Comfortable easy chairs, open fires, magazines and books bid you relax. "Farthings" as coins may long be extinct but the warmth of the welcome at this Farthings is anything but extinct!

OPEN: *All year*
NO. ROOMS: *6* EN SUITE *6*
ROOM TELEPHONES: *Yes* TV IN ROOMS: *Yes*
PETS: *Yes* CHILDREN: *Yes*
DISABLED: *Unsuitable*
LOCATION: *Off A358 between M5 and A303*

SWIMMING POOL/HEALTH CLUB: *No*
CONFERENCE FACILITIES:
Small Business Meetings up to 25
PRICE GUIDE:
SINGLE: *£80/£100* DOUBLE: *£100/£125*

Tarn Hows Hotel

Hawkshead, Ambleside, Cumbria LA22 0PR
Tel: 05394 36696 · Fax: 05394 36766

All the magic of Lakeland is bound up in the title of this highly individual hotel, surrounded by a necklace of glittering water, woods and mountains. Total restoration and re-furbishment in 1991 by owners Alan and Karen Campbell has resulted in one of the finest hotels in the Lake District. Luxurious bedrooms, charming public rooms, a superb fitness centre and full conference facilities are just some of the attractions, but it perhaps for the quality of its distinctive cuisine created by chef Kevin Cape, that Tarn Hows is becoming justly renowned.

OPEN: **All year**
NO. ROOMS: **19** EN SUITE **19**
ROOM TELEPHONES: **Yes** TV IN ROOMS: **Yes**
PETS: **By arrangement** CHILDREN: **Yes**
DISABLED: **Yes**
LOCATION: **Take A593 Coniston Rd and over Rothay Bridge**

HEALTH CLUB: **Leisure Facilities**
CONFERENCE FACILITIES:
Small Business Meetings up to 19
PRICE GUIDE:
SINGLE: **£44** DOUBLE: **£88**

The Bel Alp House

Haytor, Nr Bovey Tracey, S. Devon TQ13 9XX
Tel: 0364 661217 · Fax: 0364 661292

Glorious views across Dartmoor to the sea 20 miles away are obtained from this exquisite Edwardian Mansion. Owned and operated by Roger and Sarah Curnock, it is one of the West Country's finest and most elegant small hotels. Lovely interiors have attractive arches, stained glass windows, antiques, paintings, open fires and luxurious furnishings. Enchanting bedrooms are designed with great flair with fine fabrics and soft colours and have superb bathrooms. Sarah is responsible for the succulent food enhanced by fine crystal, silver and Wedgewood china, and from every window that magical Devonshire countryside.

OPEN: **March to November**
NO. ROOMS: **9** EN SUITE **9**
ROOM TELEPHONES: **Yes** TV IN ROOMS: **Yes**
PETS: **By arrangement**
CHILDREN: **By arrangement**
LOCATION: **2¹/2 miles from Bovey Tracey off road to Haytor (B3387)**

DISABLED: **Unsuitable**
SWIMMING POOL/HEALTH CLUB: **No**
CONFERENCE FACILITIES: **No**
PRICE GUIDE:
SINGLE: **£69/£87** DOUBLE: **£126/£150**

Holly Lodge

Heacham, King's Lynn, Norfolk PE30 7HY
Tel: 0485 70790

This 16th century listed building with its tall Elizabethan chimneys is owned and operated in a very individual way by Lesley Piper, whose home it is. Interesting bedrooms, two with 4-posters, have antique furnishings and are most appealing. In the intimate atmosphere of her candle-lit Restaurant, food of exceptional standard is artistically presented by Chef Robert Harrison. Menus are small ... and all the better for it! Breakfasts too are superb with fresh orange juice, good coffee, home-made marmalade and croissants.

OPEN: **March to December**
NO. ROOMS: **6** EN SUITE **6**
ROOM TELEPHONES: **No** TV IN ROOMS: **No**
PETS: **No** CHILDREN: **By Arrangement**
DISABLED: **Unsuitable**

SWIMMING POOL/HEALTH CLUB: **No**
CONFERENCE FACILITIES:
No
PRICE GUIDE:
SINGLE: **£55** DOUBLE: **£75/£85**

LOCATION: **Turn off A149 into Heacham at Norfolk Lavender signed left**

The Pheasant Hotel

Harome, Helmsley, N. Yorkshire T06 5JG
Tel: 0439 71241

If one were to be asked to produce a representation of olde England, the village pond, millstream and beyond, the erstwhile village blacksmiths that is now The Pheasant, would fit the bill perfectly. Sympathetic and imaginative restoration by the owners, the Binks family, has created a most charming retreat. Fresh garden produce forms the basis of the appetising English food which is the province of Mrs Tricia Binks. With its oak beams, log fires and Terrace overlooking the millstream you will enjoy this delightful hotel.

OPEN: **Early March to Mid-December**
NO. ROOMS: **12** EN SUITE **12**
ROOM TELEPHONES: **Yes** TV IN ROOMS: **Yes**
PETS: **By arrangement** CHILDREN: **Over 12**
DISABLED: **Yes**

SWIMMING POOL/HEALTH CLUB: **No**
CONFERENCE FACILITIES: **No**
PRICE GUIDE:
SINGLE: **£48/£56**
DOUBLE: **£96/£112**

The Feversham Arms

Helmsley, N. Yorkshire YO6 5AG
Tel: 0439 70766 · Fax: 0439 70346

If the Earl of Feversham could return today to the hostelry he built in 1855, he would have a surprise. Owned and operated by the Aragues family, the hotel is furnished and equipped to high standards. Bedrooms, some with 4-posters, have excellent bathrooms, each one individual in design and decor and with every conceivable extra. There is a superb Swimming Pool and all weather hard Tennis Court. Candle-lit dinners, log fires and friendly atmosphere bid you welcome when you return at the day's end.

OPEN: **All year**
NO. ROOMS: **18** EN SUITE **18**
ROOM TELEPHONES: **Yes** TV IN ROOMS: **Yes**
PETS: **Yes** CHILDREN: **Yes**
DISABLED: **Yes**
LOCATION: **Off A170**

SWIMMING POOL:
Outdoor Heated April to October
CONFERENCE FACILITIES:
Small Business Meetings up to 30
PRICE GUIDE: SINGLE: **£50/£60** DOUBLE: **£70/£80**
Bonanza Breaks Din/B&B from £40.50 p pers

Phyllis Court Club

Marlow Road, Henley-on-Thames, Oxfordshire RG9 2HT
Tel: 0491 574366 · Fax: 0491 410725

Step through the classic entrance doors and you enter a glamorous world of tinkling tea-cups, exquisitely proportioned rooms and old fashioned standards of courtesy and service you might have thought had gone for ever ... very Noël Coward! In a glorious situation on the banks of the river in fashionable Henley in its own flawless gardens which sweep down to the water, staying at "The Club" confers many benefits. Not least superb food at absurdly low prices, luxurious bedrooms and un-rivalled leisure facilities. Steeped in history, Phyllis Court can trace its origins back to 1301.

OPEN: **All year**
NO. ROOMS: **11** EN SUITE **11**
ROOM TELEPHONES: **Yes** TV IN ROOMS: **Yes**
PETS: **No** CHILDREN: **Yes**
DISABLED: **By Arrangement**
LOCATION: **On A4155 Marlow Road at junction of Oxford Road**

SWIMMING POOL/HEALTH CLUB: **No**
CONFERENCE FACILITIES: **Up to 11 Resident Theatre Style up to 250**
PRICE GUIDE: SINGLE: **From £66.50**
DOUBLE: **From £87**

Nuthurst Grange

Hockley Heath, Warwickshire B94 5NL
Tel: 0564 783972 · Fax: 0564 783919

This delightful hotel immediately conveys an air of repose and comfort. The appealing public rooms are intimate and snug. Luxurious bedrooms have a host of extras, like fresh flowers, fruit, chocolate home-made biscuits and superb whirlpool bath in all bathrooms. Chef Proprietor David Randolph and his team of talented chefs produce memorable dishes, classical French and traditional English, all based on fresh produce. Set in over 7 acres of lovely gardens with its own Heli-Pad, the Grange makes an ideal base whether on business or pleasure.

OPEN: **All year**
NO. ROOMS: **15** EN SUITE **15**
ROOM TELEPHONES: **Yes** TV IN ROOMS: **Yes**
PETS: **By arrangement** CHILDREN: **Yes**
DISABLED: **Non Residents for Dining**
LOCATION: **Off Jcn 4 on M42, take A3400 through Hockley Heath, lane 1/2 mile on right**

SWIMMING POOL/HEALTH CLUB: **No**
CONFERENCE FACILITIES:
Theatre Style up to 80
PRICE GUIDE:
SINGLE: **£89** DOUBLE: **£99/£135**

Combe House Hotel

Gittisham, Nr Honiton, Devon EX14 0AD
Tel: 0404 42756 · Fax: 0404 46004

This Elizabethan Mansion, dating from the 14th century lies within its own glorious grounds and commands extensive views of the lush Devonshire countryside. Owned and operated by the Boswell family, Combe House conveys the atmosphere of more gracious days. one might be a member of a house party. A roaring fire burns in the Great Hall in winter. There are two Dining Rooms. one with a superb Rococco Fireplace with mirrored overmantle. the other has a fine Italian fireplace and muralled walls by Theresa Boswell. Food is of exceptional standard with good coffee. Ancestral portraits, a cosy bar hung with photographs of the family's racehorses, a real home.

OPEN: **All year**
NO. ROOMS: **15** EN SUITE **15**
ROOM TELEPHONES: **Yes** TV IN ROOMS: **Yes**
PETS: **Yes** CHILDREN: **Yes**
DISABLED: **Unsuitable**
LOCATION: **Turn off A30 westbound side of dual carriageway signposted Gittisham**

SWIMMING POOL/HEALTH CLUB: **No**
CONFERENCE FACILITIES:
Small Business Meetings up to 12
PRICE GUIDE: SINGLE: **£62.50/£92.50**
DOUBLE: **£95/£123.50**

Petersfield House Hotel

Horning, Norfolk NR12 8PF
Tel: 0692 630741 · Fax: 0692 630745

Owned and operated in a very friendly fashion by Philip and Gwen Crouch and their son Robin, this pleasing hotel nestles in its own tranquil grounds in the heart of the Norfolk Broads. You can enjoy really excellent food in the impressively proportioned Restaurant which overlooks the garden with its lily pond and fountain. Petersfield House is one of that rare breed of rapidly diminishing hotels which offers real value for money.

OPEN: *All year*
NO. ROOMS: *18* EN SUITE *18*
ROOM TELEPHONES: *Yes* TV IN ROOMS: *Yes*
PETS: *Yes* CHILDREN: *Yes*
DISABLED: *Unsuitable*
LOCATION: *From Wroxham turn off A1062 to Horning*

SWIMMING POOL/HEALTH CLUB: *No*
CONFERENCE FACILITIES:
Small Business Meetings up to 40
PRICE GUIDE:
SINGLE: *£60* DOUBLE: *£75*

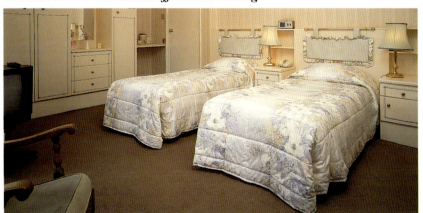

Rombalds

West View, Wells Road, Ilkley, W. Yorkshire LS29 9JG
Tel: 0943 603201 · Fax: 0943 816586

It is rare to find a small hotel that excels in so many ways as does this oasis of good living at the gateway to the Moors. Rombalds has established an international reputation for its outstanding cuisine, which has won many accolades. Bedrooms are comfortable with a host of extras. But for the businessman you enter a fantasy world of high-tech presentation facilities in the Coach House Boardroom. Owned by Ian and Jill Guthrie, Rombalds is unique in the sheer range of services it offers to all, even to a dining club and two luxury service flats.

OPEN: ***All year***
NO. ROOMS: ***15*** EN SUITE ***15***
ROOM TELEPHONES: ***Yes*** TV IN ROOMS: ***Yes***
PETS: ***Yes*** CHILDREN: ***Yes***
DISABLED: ***Hotel unsuitable/***
    Restaurant suitable

SWIMMING POOL/HEALTH CLUB: ***No***
CONFERENCE FACILITIES:
Small Business Meetings up to 50
PRICE GUIDE: SINGLE: ***£63/£86***
DOUBLE: ***£92/£108*** SUITES: ***£124/152***

The Commodore

Marine Parade, Instow, N. Devon EX39 4JN
Tel: 0271 860347 · Fax: 0271 861233

This gleaming white, immaculately maintained marine hotel situated virtually on the water's edge has a very Mediterranean feel. Owned and operated by the very welcoming Woolaway family, public rooms are most pleasing with their elegant proportions and quality furnishings. The Restaurant presents inventive food from a talented brigade of chefs. Local produce features prominently on the extensive menus. Some of the well designed bedrooms have their own sea facing balconies. Summer days, Devonshire Cream Teas on the Sun Terrace ... what could be better?

OPEN: **All year**
NO. ROOMS: **24** EN SUITE **24**
ROOM TELEPHONES: **Yes** TV IN ROOMS: **Yes**
PETS: **No** CHILDREN: **Over 12**
DISABLED: **Yes**

SWIMMING POOL/HEALTH CLUB: **No**
CONFERENCE FACILITIES:
Theatre style up to 300
PRICE GUIDE:
SINGLE: **£55/£65** DOUBLE: **£82/£98**

LOCATION: **Turn off M5 at Junction 27 to Link Road and follow Instow signs**

Belstead Brook Hotel

Belstead Road, Ipswich, Suffolk IP2 9HB
Tel: 0473 684241 · Fax: 0473 681249

This luxurious hotel set in 8 acres of delightful grounds has been totally transformed to combine 20th century facilities with 16th century charm. From the comfort of the lounge bar to the oak panelled atmosphere of the Jacobean restaurant to the appealing bedrooms (some with whirlpool baths and 4-posters) Belstead Brook makes a perfect base for business or pleasure. Courteous, professional staff ensure your comfort. Companies will be delighted with the purpose built syndicate rooms.

OPEN: **All year**
NO. ROOMS: **91** EN SUITE **91**
ROOM TELEPHONES: **Yes** TV IN ROOMS: **Yes**
PETS: **No** CHILDREN: **Yes**
DISABLED: **Yes**

SWIMMING POOL/HEALTH CLUB: **No**
CONFERENCE FACILITIES:
Business Meetings up to 60
PRICE GUIDE: SINGLE: **£59.50**
DOUBLE: **£69.50 (Room only)**

St. Martins Hotel

Island of St. Martins, Isles of Scilly
Tel: 0720 22092 · Fax 0720 22298

And now as they say, for something completely different! where the "rush hour" is likely to be the passing of a couple of small boats. Glittering azure waters and white beaches of the finest sand surround this unique hotel. Owner Robert Francis and his wife Theresa have created a luxury hotel on an island paradise. Beautifully designed bedrooms and suites look towards Tresco and Round Island Lighthouse. Delicate pastel fabrics and designer decor result in an elegant ambience. Superb food is served in the lovely Dining Room with its stunning dramatic panorama of islands, sea and sand. There's a delicious amount of nothing to do at St. Martins, truly … "the ultimate escape".

OPEN: **March to end October**
NO. ROOMS: **24** EN SUITE **24**
ROOM TELEPHONES: **Yes** TV IN ROOMS: **Yes**
PETS: **Yes** CHILDREN: **Yes**
DISABLED: **Yes**
LOCATION: **Island of St. Martins**

SWIMMING POOL: **Yes**
CONFERENCE FACILITIES:
Small Business Meetings – Director level
PRICE GUIDE:
SINGLE: **£65/£105** DOUBLE: **£130/£210**

Winterbourne Hotel

Bonchurch, Isle of Wight PO38 1RQ
Tel: 0983 852535 · Fax: 0983 853056

This has to be the most beautiful setting on the Island. Enchanting gardens ablaze with colour in season contain a waterfall and stream, with the blue waters of the bay beyond. A private path leads to a small beach. Owners Mr & Mrs Pat O'Connor will welcome you with genuine warmth to their attractive hotel, once the home of Charles Dickens. In the period atmosphere of the candle-lit Regency Dining Room the finest ingredients are used for the varied menus. As Dickens wrote, "the prettiest place I ever saw in my life, at home or abroad".

OPEN: **March to end November**
NO. ROOMS: **19** EN SUITE **19**
ROOM TELEPHONES: **Yes** TV IN ROOMS: **Yes**
PETS: **Yes** CHILDREN: **Yes**
DISABLED: **Unsuitable**

SWIMMING POOL: **Outdoor Heated**
CONFERENCE FACILITIES: **No**
PRICE GUIDE:
SINGLE: **£55/£64 (inc 5-course Dinner)**
DOUBLE: **£110/128 (inc 5-course Dinner)**

Jervaulx Hall

Nr Masham, Ripon, N. Yorkshire HG4 4PH
Tel: 0677 60235

This small peaceful hotel lies in a tranquil and romantic setting in its own lovely gardens adjacent to the famous Abbey Ruins. Drawing Room and Hall have open fires and are furnished with antiques. Bedrooms are cosy with fresh decor. Food is good and plentiful in the best traditions of country house cooking. Genial owners Mr & Mrs John Sharp like to create a convivial atmosphere as you will find when you gather around the communal toaster at breakfast!

OPEN: **Mid-March to end November**
NO. ROOMS: **10** EN SUITE **10**
ROOM TELEPHONES: **No** TV IN ROOMS: **No**
PETS: **Yes** CHILDREN: **Yes**
DISABLED: **Yes**
LOCATION: **Off A6108 twelve miles from Ripon**

SWIMMING POOL/HEALTH CLUB: **No**
CONFERENCE FACILITIES: **No**
PRICE GUIDE:
SINGLE: **£75 (incl Dinner)**
DOUBLE: **£120 (incl Dinner)**

Underscar Manor

Applethwaite, Keswick CA1Z 4PH
Tel: 07687 75000 · Fax: 07687 74904

Stunning is perhaps no exaggeration when applied to this elegant Italianate style country house and the views it commands across Derwentwater and the surrounding fells. Total upgrading and refurbishment in 1991 by owners Pauline and Derek Harrison and Gordon Evans has resulted in one of Lakelands most luxurious hotels. Beautifully designed bedrooms have everything the discerning guest could wish for. Superb cuisine is guaranteed since the owners have, for 17 years, run the acclaimed Moss Nook Restaurant near Manchester Airport. Of great architectural interest, Underscar takes its place as one of England's best.

OPEN: **All year**
NO. ROOMS: **11** EN SUITE **11**
ROOM TELEPHONES: **Yes** TV IN ROOMS: **Yes**
PETS: **No** CHILDREN: **Over 14**
DISABLED: **Unsuitable**

SWIMMING POOL/HEALTH CLUB: **No**
CONFERENCE FACILITIES:
Small Business Meetings up to 20
PRICE GUIDE: SINGLE: **£75/£105**
DOUBLE: **£150/£250 (incl Dinner)**

LOCATION: **Off A66 two miles North of Keswick; 17 miles from M6 Junction 40**

Armathwaite Hall Hotel

Bassenthwaite Lake, Keswick, Cumbria CA12 4RE
Tel: 07687 76551 · Fax: 07687 76220

Originally a stately home, this magnificently situated hotel standing in 400 acres of superb grounds surrounded by a panorama of mountains and lakes is all things to all men. Rooms are impressively proportioned with a wealth of fine panelling and elegant bedrooms are well appointed. Matchless facilities include: an Equestrian Centre with qualified instructors, a rare breeds farm, fishing, clay shooting, archery, tennis, snooker, etc and a superb Leisure Club with beauty therapist. Conferences are especially well catered for in a suite of 4 rooms.

OPEN: **All year**
NO. ROOMS: **42** EN SUITE **42**
ROOM TELEPHONES: **Yes** TV IN ROOMS: **Yes**
PETS: **Yes** CHILDREN: **Yes**
DISABLED: **By arrangement**
LOCATION: **Take Castle Inn junction off A591**

SWIMMING POOL/HEALTH CLUB: **Yes**
CONFERENCE FACILITIES:
Up to 100 Theatre Style
PRICE GUIDE:
SINGLE: **From £75** DOUBLE: **From £110**

Knights Hill Hotel

Knights Hill Village, King's Lynn, Norfolk PE30 3HQ
Tel: 0553 675566 · Fax: 0553 675568

This is not just another hotel but rather a unique complex of Hotel, Inn, Leisure Club and Conference Centre, with a rustic flavour, all blended together to form Knights Hill Village. The hotel has evolved from 16th century hunting lodge to a hotel of charm and character with high levels of comfort. The Inn has a wealth of beams, cobbles and open fires, whilst the Conference Centre offers companies every possible facility. With its comprehensive Leisure Club there is something to suit all tastes at Knights Hill.

OPEN: **All year**
NO. ROOMS: **54** EN SUITE **54**
ROOM TELEPHONES: **Yes** TV IN ROOMS: **Yes**
PETS: **Yes**   CHILDREN: **Yes**
DISABLED: **Yes**
LOCATION: **At intersection of A148 and A149**

SWIMMING POOL/HEALTH CLUB: **Yes**
CONFERENCE FACILITIES:
Business Meetings up to 350
PRICE GUIDE: SINGLE: **£62.50/£75**
DOUBLE: **£70/£85 (Room only)**

The Dower House

Bond End, Knaresborough, Yorkshire HG5 9AL
Tel: 0423 863302 · Fax: 0423 867665

A combination of olde world character and 20th century facilities are to be found in the comfortable bedrooms of this Grade 2 listed building nestling in its own delightful gardens. The superb Corniche Club boasts a very well equipped Gymnasium, Pool, Jacuzzi, Sauna and Steam Room. For the businessman, the new Conference Centre has a full range of audio-visual aids and secretarial services with four syndicate rooms. At the day's end excellent food and fine wines are available in the Terrace Restaurant.

OPEN: **All year**
NO. ROOMS: **32** EN SUITE **32**
ROOM TELEPHONES: **Yes** TV IN ROOMS: **Yes**
PETS: **Yes** CHILDREN: **Yes**
DISABLED: **Yes**
LOCATION: **On A59 York – Harrogate road**

SWIMMING POOL/HEALTH CLUB: **Yes**
CONFERENCE FACILITIES:
Theatre Style up to 70
PRICE GUIDE:
SINGLE: **£54.50/57** DOUBLE: **£71/75**

Sharrow Bay Country House Hotel

Ullswater, Penrith, Cumbria CA10 2LZ
Tel: 07684 86301/86483 · Fax: 07684 86349

This, the first true "Country House Hotel" is renowned world-wide for not only the superb food and elegant ambience, other hotels can claim similar, but it is the genuine warmth of welcome from owners Brian Sack and Francis Coulson that makes Sharrow that "little bit special". If space permitted I could go on about the spectacular lakeside location, the fells, the daffodils, stunning foliage, fine paintings, porcelain, luxurious bedrooms and "that food" ... but space does not permit. Most enduring of all is the 42 years of dedication by the owners which has made Sharrow Bay a legend in its lifetime.

OPEN: ***February 28th to Early December***
NO. ROOMS: 30 EN SUITE **26**
ROOM TELEPHONES: Yes TV IN ROOMS: **Yes**
PETS: No CHILDREN: ***Over 13***
DISABLED: Unsuitable
SWIMMING POOL/HEALTH CLUB: ***No***
CONFERENCE FACILITIES:
Small Business Meetings up to 12
PRICE GUIDE: SINGLE: **£123**
DOUBLE: **£290 (incl Dinner & Full Breakfast)**
LOCATION: *Off A592 into Pooley Bridge and then Howtown Road for two miles*

Langdale Chase

Windermere, Cumbria, LA23 1LW
Tel: 05394 32201 · Fax: 05394 32604

It would be difficult to imagine a more beautiful and idyllic situation than the one enjoyed by this lovely Country House Hotel nestling on the shores of Lake Windermere with the Langdale Pikes beyond. Reflecting a more gracious age, Langdale Chase combines charm and elegance with 20th century appointments. Superb oak panelling and paintings grace the mellow Great Hall. Each bedroom has its own character and has been furnished with great taste. Exquisite gardens lead to a romantic boat-house with bedroom above, with its own rose Langdale Chase is undoubtedly one of Lakeland's most delightful hotels.

OPEN: **All year**
NO. ROOMS: **31** EN SUITE **31**
ROOM TELEPHONES: **Yes** TV IN ROOMS: **Yes**
PETS: **Yes** CHILDREN: **Yes**
DISABLED: **Yes**
LOCATION: **Off A591 Windermere to Ambleside road**

SWIMMING POOL/HEALTH CLUB: **No**
CONFERENCE FACILITIES:
Small Business Meetings up to 15
PRICE GUIDE:
SINGLE: **From £52** DOUBLE: **From £104**

Langar Hall

Langar, Nottingham NG13 9HG
Tel: 0949 60559 · Fax: 0949 61045

More a home than an hotel, this tranquil house nestling close to the church is owned and operated, with charming mild eccentricity, by Imogen Skirving. Situated in the unspoilt Vale of Belvoir, the house is a favourite haunt of many notables from the media and from as far back as the thirties has played host to many famous names from the world of cricket, both players and commentators. Antiques, paintings, log fires, individual bedrooms and creative cuisine served in a pillared dining room combine in an atmosphere of warmth and welcome.

OPEN: ***All year***
NO. ROOMS: ***12*** EN SUITE ***12***
ROOM TELEPHONES: ***Yes*** TV IN ROOMS: ***Yes***
PETS: ***Yes*** CHILDREN: ***Yes***
DISABLED: ***Unsuitable***
LOCATION: ***Behind the Church***

SWIMMING POOL/HEALTH CLUB: ***No***
CONFERENCE FACILITIES:
Small Business Meetings up to 20
PRICE GUIDE:
SINGLE: ***£50*** DOUBLE: ***£50/£98***

Lastingham Grange

Lastingham, York YO6 6TH
Tel: 07515 345 & 402

I believe it was the poet W.B. Yeats who spoke of "peace dropping slow", he might well have had the setting of Lastingham Grange in mind. It would be difficult to imagine a more tranquil and idyllic location. Its own ten acres of beautifully tended gardens are surrounded by stone walls, sheep, and beyond, the dramatic back-drop of the Moors. Owned and loved by the Wood family, this reposeful Country House Hotel embodies all that is best in the way of traditional English values ... good food, comfort and courteous service.

OPEN: **March to end November**
NO. ROOMS: **12** EN SUITE **12**
ROOM TELEPHONES: **Yes** TV IN ROOMS: **Yes**
PETS: **Yes** CHILDREN: **Yes**
DISABLED: **Unsuitable**
LOCATION: **Off A170 Helmsley – Pickering road**

SWIMMING POOL/HEALTH CLUB: **No**
CONFERENCE FACILITIES:
No
PRICE GUIDE:
SINGLE: **£59** DOUBLE: **£109**

Haley's Hotel & Restaurant

Shire Oak Road, Headingly, Leeds LS6 2DE
Tel: 0532 784446 · Fax: 0532 753342

This fine Victorian house is the very epitome of elegance and charm. Step inside and you enter a world of style and opulence. Rich drapes and tastefully colour co-ordinated furnishings create a feeling of repose from the turbulent world outside. Food is of particular importance at Haley's, chef Andrew Foster is developing a considerable reputation for his imaginative cooking. Breakfasts are superb! With an air-conditioned meeting room, individual bedrooms and old fashioned standards of service, Haley's is indeed a connoisseurs choice.

OPEN: **All year**
NO. ROOMS: **22** EN SUITE **22**
ROOM TELEPHONES: **Yes** TV IN ROOMS: **Yes**
PETS: **No** CHILDREN: **Yes**
DISABLED: **Unsuitable**
LOCATION: **2 miles north of City Centre off A660**

SWIMMING POOL/HEALTH CLUB: **No**
CONFERENCE FACILITIES:
Small Business Meetings up to 25
PRICE GUIDE:
SINGLE: **£95** DOUBLE: **£112** SUITES: **£165**

42 The Calls

42 The Calls, Leeds, West Yorkshire LS2 7EW
Tel: 0532 440099 · Fax: 0532 344100

"Vive La Difference" might well be the slogan for this highly original designer inspired hotel right at the heart of Leeds city centre. Unique is often an overworked adjective, but not when applied to this Quixotic former grain mill overlooking the canal. Singular bedrooms are the ultimate for the discerning businessman with 3 telephones, desk, satellite TV and stereo. Secretarial facilities and fax are available and there are even private breakfast hatches. In the ambience of a riverside setting, jaded guests will appreciate the luxury of such individual and appealing bedrooms.

OPEN: **All year**
NO. ROOMS: **39** EN SUITE **39**
ROOM TELEPHONES: **Yes** TV IN ROOMS: **Yes**
PETS: **No** CHILDREN: **Yes**
DISABLED: **Yes**

SWIMMING POOL/HEALTH CLUB: **No**
CONFERENCE FACILITIES:
Small Business Meetings from 5 to 50
PRICE GUIDE: SINGLE: **£95/£125** DOUBLE:
£100 (Room only) SUITES: **£140/£185**

LOCATION: **From M1 Jcn 46 head for Harrogate turn right at Tetleys Brewery over bridge & 1st left**

Lewtrenchard Manor

Lewdown, Nr Okehampton, Devon EX20 4PN
Tel: 056683 256 or 222 · Fax: 056683 332

This beautiful atmospheric Manor House dating from 1620 is now one of Devonshire's finest Country House Hotels. You may arrive feeling harassed and fraught but it will not be long before the timeless tranquillity of this old house works it magic on you. Mellow oak panelling, great open fireplaces, lovely stained glass windows, elaborate ceilings and original oils grace public rooms. Bedrooms some with 4-posters, are charming and restful with delightful views. Lewtrenchard has attained a considerable reputation for the excellence of its cuisine and is under the supervision of owners James and Sue Murray whose home this is.

OPEN: **All year (except 3 weeks Jan/Feb)**
NO. ROOMS: **8** EN SUITE **8**
ROOM TELEPHONES: **Yes** TV IN ROOMS: **Yes**
PETS: **Yes** CHILDREN: **Over 8**
DISABLED: **Unsuitable**
LOCATION: **Turn off A30 at Lewdown and then ¾ mile on left**

SWIMMING POOL/HEALTH CLUB: **No**
CONFERENCE FACILITIES:
Small Business Meetings
PRICE GUIDE:
SINGLE: **£75/£95** DOUBLE: **£95/£130**

The Arundell Arms

Lifton, Devon PL16 0AA
Tel: 0566 784666 · Fax: 0566 784494

This old Coaching Inn, whose origins date from Saxon times, is renowned as one of England's premier fishing hotels with 20 miles of its own water on the River Tamar. A constant programme of upgrading by the owner Anne Voss-Bark has resulted in a delightful Cocktail Bar and elegant Dining Room with its designer drapes, crystal chandeliers and superb food. English and French dishes are presented with flair. An open fire burns in the Lounge and you will have a good bed in rooms which are equipped with thoughtful extras like fresh flowers on arrival. An ideal base for touring the West Country.

OPEN: *All year*
NO. ROOMS: *24* EN SUITE *24*
ROOM TELEPHONES: *Yes* TV IN ROOMS: *Yes*
PETS: *Yes* CHILDREN: *Yes*
DISABLED: *Unsuitable*

SWIMMING POOL/HEALTH CLUB:
No
CONFERENCE FACILITIES:
Business Meetings up to 100
PRICE GUIDE: SINGLE: *£60* DOUBLE: *£90*

LOCATION: *Half mile from A30 forty miles west of Exeter and M5 in Lifton Village*

The Basil Street Hotel

Knightsbridge, London SW3 1AH
Tel: 071 581 3311 · Fax: 071 581 3693

Old fashioned standards of courtesy and service still apply at this Edwardian hotel (191 steps from Harrods), one of the few privately owned hotels left in London. An elegant Georgian staircase ascends to comfortable bedrooms. "The Basil" is a peaceful "home from home" for visitors from all over the world who recognise in it a human alternative to the bland anonymity of the hotel chains. Good food is served by smiling waiters in the pleasant Dining Room, accompanied each evening by live piano music played by a member of the Royal College of Music.

OPEN: *All year*
NO. ROOMS: *92* EN SUITE *82*
ROOM TELEPHONES: *Yes* TV IN ROOMS: *Yes*
PETS: *Yes* CHILDREN: *Yes*
DISABLED: *Unsuitable*
LOCATION: *Near Harrods in Basil Street*

SWIMMING POOL/HEALTH CLUB: *No*
CONFERENCE FACILITIES:
Business Meetings up to 50
PRICE GUIDE: SINGLE: *From £105.25*
DOUBLE: *From £149*

Halcyon Hotel

81 Holland Park, London W11 3RZ
Tel: 071 727 7288 · Fax: 071 229 8516

I have heard film stars wax lyrical about The Halcyon, asserting it to be "the finest hotel in London". Sumptuous bedrooms and suites are strikingly individual, all air-conditioned and with splendid marble bathrooms, some having Jacuzzi baths. The enchanting Restaurant has three French windows opening onto a captivating ornamental garden and patio, a setting to match the creative cuisine and fine wines. For connoisseurs of good living the consummate elegance of this exquisite town house should prove irresistible.

OPEN: **All year**
NO. ROOMS: **44** EN SUITE **44**
ROOM TELEPHONES: **Yes** TV IN ROOMS: **Yes**
PETS: **No** CHILDREN: **Yes**
DISABLED: **Unsuitable**

SWIMMING POOL/HEALTH CLUB: **No**
CONFERENCE FACILITIES:
Small Business Meetings up to 12
PRICE GUIDE:
SINGLE: **£165** DOUBLE: **£185/£300**

The Abbey Court Hotel

20, Pembridge Gardens, London W2 4DU
Tel: 071-221 7518 · Fax: 071-727 5815

Privately owned and operated by professional hoteliers, Mr & Mrs Yazim Nanji, this Victorian town house offers high standards of accommodation in individually designed bedrooms. Some of the rooms have 4-poster beds. Bathrooms are excellent with many thoughtful extras, some having whirlpool baths. Although there is no restaurant, snacks are available via 24 hour room service. Furnished with antiques, original paintings and unique mirrors, this small personally run establishment represents good value for money.

OPEN: **All year**
NO. ROOMS: **22** EN SUITE **22**
ROOM TELEPHONES: **Yes** TV IN ROOMS: **Yes**
PETS: **No** CHILDREN: **Under 1 yr & over 12**
DISABLED: **Unsuitable**

SWIMMING POOL/HEALTH CLUB: **No**
CONFERENCE FACILITIES:
Small Business Meetings up to 20
PRICE GUIDE: SINGLE: **£90** DOUBLE: **£130**
4-POSTER: **£160 Special Corporate rate available (Room only)**

Linden Hall

Longhorsley, Morpeth, Northumberland NE65 8XF
Tel: 0670 516611 · Fax: 0670 88544

This impressive Grade 2 listed Georgian Country House Hotel refers to itself as "grand but not stuffy" which is a fair description. Situated in its own 300 acres, its elegant public rooms have all the period atmosphere of the great English Country Houses, with antiques, fine fireplaces, paintings, a magnificent staircase and various objects d'art. Bedrooms are supremely comfortable, some having 4-posters with every conceivable extra. Food is notable as are the excellent breakfasts. Facilities (too many to detail) include: Beauty Salon, Sauna, Solarium, Snooker, Clay Shooting, Croquet, Fishing, Tennis. Truly a self-contained world of its own and one of the major hotels of the North East.

OPEN: **All year**
NO. ROOMS: **55** EN SUITE **55**
ROOM TELEPHONES: **Yes** TV IN ROOMS: **Yes**
PETS: **Yes** CHILDREN: **Yes**
DISABLED: **Yes**
LOCATION: **On A697 north of Longhorsley**

SWIMMING POOL/HEALTH CLUB: **Yes and Health and Beauty Spa**
CONFERENCE FACILITIES: **From 10 to 300**
PRICE GUIDE: SINGLE: FROM **£92.50**
DOUBLE: **From £115**
2 nights DBB from £150 per person

Dinham Hall

Dinham, Ludlow, Shropshire SY8 1EJ
Tel: 0584 876464 · Fax: 0584 876019

A relaxed friendly atmosphere is immediately apparent as you enter this charming small hotel, which dates from 1792 and lies a few steps from the castle. In the elegant Restaurant, subtle pastel decor and soft lighting complement innovative cooking which has won many accolades for Dinham Hall. The bedrooms are traditionally furnished and in keeping with the rest of the Hall, harmonious design giving a restful feel throughout. For the active there is a comprehensively equipped Gymnasium and Sauna.

OPEN: **All year**
NO. ROOMS: **14** EN SUITE **14**
ROOM TELEPHONES: **Yes** TV IN ROOMS: **Yes**
PETS: **Yes** CHILDREN: **Yes**
DISABLED: **Unsuitable**
LOCATION: **By the Castle**

SWIMMING POOL/HEALTH CLUB: **No**
CONFERENCE FACILITIES:
Small Business Meetings up to 24
PRICE GUIDE: SINGLE: **£49.50/£60.50**
DOUBLE: **£76/£97.50**

The Stanwell House Hotel

High Street, Lymington, Hampshire SO41 9AA
Tel: 0590 677123 · Fax: 0590 677756

A "country house in town" but this is no ordinary town. This is a town of bobbing boats, giant ocean racers, yachts, dorys, bustling marinas and all the vivid life of the waterfront. At its heart lies this charming hotel, an oasis of relaxed comfort. Stanwell House has a very intimate air with its cosy public rooms with quality furnishings and attractive decor. Bedrooms are equally appealing, well appointed with good bathrooms, whilst in the unusually named Railings Restaurant, fresh produce forms the basis of varied menus.

OPEN: *All year*
NO. ROOMS: *35* EN SUITE *35*
ROOM TELEPHONES: *Yes* TV IN ROOMS: *Yes*
PETS: *No* CHILDREN: *Yes*
DISABLED: *Unsuitable*

SWIMMING POOL/HEALTH CLUB: *No*
CONFERENCE FACILITIES:
Small Business Meetings up to 25
PRICE GUIDE:
SINGLE: *£72.50* DOUBLE: *£98*

Passford House Hotel

Mount Pleasant, Nr Lymington, Hants SO41 8LS
Tel: 0590 682398 · Fax: 0590 683494

On the fringe of the Forest, this is a fine hotel with a relaxed atmosphere and courteous and efficient staff. There are numerous comfortable lounges, one with oak panelling and open fire in bad weather. Food is of excellent standard and is served in a most attractive Dining Room. Bedrooms vary from comfortable to luxurious and have every modern facility. The Dolphin Leisure Centre has Swimming Pool, Spa Pool, Sauna, Solarium and Multi-Gym. Passford House is owned and operated by Mr and Mrs Patrick Heritage.

OPEN: **All year**
NO. ROOMS: **50** EN SUITE **50**
ROOM TELEPHONES: **Yes** TV IN ROOMS: **Yes**
PETS: **Yes** CHILDREN: **Yes**
DISABLED: **Yes**
LOCATION: **Two miles north west of Lymington off A337**

SWIMMING POOL: **Yes 2 pools and leisure complex**
CONFERENCE FACILITIES:
Small Business Meetings up to 30-40
PRICE GUIDE: SINGLE: **£75** DOUBLE: **£107**

The Lynton Cottage Hotel

Northwalk Hill, Lynton, N. Devon EX35 6ED
Tel: 0598 52342 · Fax: 0598 52597

Superbly positioned commanding un-rivalled vistas of Exmoor and Lynmouth Bay, this former residence of a Knight of the Realm offers today's travellers high standards of creature comfort. Owner John Jones has created an elegant and luxurious hotel where award winning chefs present menus to satisfy the most discerning. All bedrooms (some with 4-posters) are furnished with taste and style and have quality fittings, all have excellent bathrooms. It's therapeutic just to sit on the Sun Terrace soaking up the endless tranquillity.

OPEN: **February to end December**
NO. ROOMS: **17** EN SUITE **17**
ROOM TELEPHONES: **Yes** TV IN ROOMS: **Yes**
PETS: **By arrangement** CHILDREN: **Over 10**
DISABLED: **Unsuitable**
LOCATION: **In town centre hotel is signed beside church**

SWIMMING POOL/HEALTH CLUB: **No**
CONFERENCE FACILITIES:
Small Business Meetings up to 18
PRICE GUIDE:
SINGLE: **£50/£65** DOUBLE: **£100/£130**

Fredrick's Hotel and Restaurant

Shoppenhangers Road, Maidenhead, Berkshire SL6 2PZ
Tel: 0628 35934 · Fax: 0628 771054

The dream of proprietor Fredrick Losel is to "create the finest in cuisine, comfort and thoughtful service". How well he has succeeded you can judge for yourself. Strikingly individual - unashamedly luxurious. From the stunning Dining Room where only the finest ingredients are used to produce matchless cuisine, to glamorous bedroom suites, stylish, elegant, and the last word in comfort, to unique flower filled public areas, all this is Fredrick's ... and much more ... so much more!

OPEN: ***All year (except 24th to 30th Dec)***
NO. ROOMS: **37** EN SUITE **37**
ROOM TELEPHONES: **Yes** TV IN ROOMS: **Yes**
PETS: **No** CHILDREN: **Yes**
DISABLED: ***Unsuitable***
LOCATION: ***Close to exit of Jcn 8/9 on M4***

SWIMMING POOL/HEALTH CLUB: **No**
CONFERENCE FACILITIES:
Theatre Style up to 100
PRICE GUIDE:
SINGLE: ***£120/£130*** DOUBLE: ***£155/£165***

The Old Bell Hotel

Abbey Row, Malmesbury, Wilts SN16 0BW
Tel: 0666 822344 · Fax: 0666 825145

This Grade 1 listed building is a positive mecca for lovers of antiquity. Possibly England's oldest hotel, its origins date back to the reign of King John. Massive oak beams dominate some of the atmospheric bedrooms, many with 4-posters, all very comfortable. Particularly noteworthy is the 100 year old wisteria which cloaks the hotel front, while to the rear is an idyllic old English garden with its flowers, roses, trees, old walls and even a Gazebo. Here in the land of King Athelstan with its Norman Abbey, creature comforts at the Old Bell are anything but "ancient"!

OPEN: ***All year***
NO. ROOMS: ***37*** EN SUITE ***37***
ROOM TELEPHONES: ***Yes*** TV IN ROOMS: ***Yes***
PETS: ***No*** CHILDREN: ***Yes***
DISABLED: ***Unsuitable***

SWIMMING POOL/HEALTH CLUB: ***No***
CONFERENCE FACILITIES:
Small Business Meetings up to 25
PRICE GUIDE: SINGLE: ***£72.50***
DOUBLE: ***£98***

Whatley Manor

Easton Grey, Malmesbury, Wiltshire SN16 0RB
Tel: 0666 822888 · Fax: 0666 826120

A supreme example of a fine Cotswold Manor. Grand but not stuffy, the atmosphere is relaxed and friendly. There is a stunning Drawing Room, magnificently proportioned with a wealth of oak panelling and cheerful log fire, a panelled Entrance Hall also with log fire, Library, and elegant Dining Room offering the best of country house cooking. Bedrooms (some with 4-posters) are furnished in keeping with the period nature of the house. Outstanding Leisure facilities include: Swimming Pool, Sauna, Solarium Jacuzzi, Croquet, Snooker, Table Tennis and all weather Tennis Court.

OPEN: **All year**
NO. ROOMS: **29** EN SUITE **29**
ROOM TELEPHONES: **Yes** TV IN ROOMS: **Yes**
PETS: **Yes** CHILDREN: **Yes**
DISABLED: **Unsuitable**
LOCATION: **Off B4040 Malmesbury – Easton Grey Road**

SWIMMING POOL: **Yes**
CONFERENCE FACILITIES:
Small Business Meetings up to 25
PRICE GUIDE:
SINGLE: **£82** DOUBLE: **£130**

The Cottage in the Wood

Holywell Road, Malvern Wells, Worcestershire WR14 4LG
Tel: 0684 573487 · Fax: 0684 560662

This charmingly named hotel commands one of the most extensive views in England. Perched high in the Malvern Hills (famous as the home of Sire Edward Elgar) one's eyes are carried to distant horizons across a beautiful valley. Inside, a cosy lounge and bar open onto the sun terrace and have open fires in winter. The attractive restaurant enjoys the same fabulous views and serves good English fare backed by an unusual wine list. Comfortable bedrooms, some with 4-posters, are well appointed. Owned and operated by John & Sue Pattin, the hotel is perfectly situated for touring the Wye Valley, the Welsh Marches and Cotswolds.

OPEN: **All year**
NO. ROOMS: **20** EN SUITE **20**
ROOM TELEPHONES: **Yes** TV IN ROOMS: **Yes**
PETS: **Yes** CHILDREN: **Yes**
DISABLED: **Unsuitable**

SWIMMING POOL/HEALTH CLUB: **No**
CONFERENCE FACILITIES:
Small Business Meetings up to 14
PRICE GUIDE:
SINGLE: **£57** DOUBLE: **£89/£125**
LOCATION: **Off A449 3 miles south of Malvern opposite Jet Filling Station**

Budock Vean

Mawnan Smith, Falmouth, S. Cornwall TR11 5LG
Tel: 0326 250288 · Fax: 0326 250892

Sixty five acres of lovely sub-tropical grounds including a Golf Course, surround this sporting Country House Hotel and reach down to the romantic Helford River, the setting for Daphne Du Mauriers Frenchmans Creek. There is a unique indoor Swimming Pool with a canopied poolside log fire, and all weather Tennis Courts. Major up-grading and re-furbishment brings the bedrooms up to international standards, some have 4-posters, most superb views across the gardens to the river beyond. Log fires burn in winter whilst in the lofty Dining Room, local Cornish produce features on varied menus. Staff are courteous and welcoming.

OPEN: **Mid-February to early New Year**
NO. ROOMS: **58** EN SUITE **58**
ROOM TELEPHONES: **Yes** TV IN ROOMS: **Yes**
PETS: **Yes** CHILDREN: **Yes**
DISABLED: **Unsuitable**
LOCATION: **Through Mawnan Smith and then signposted from Helford Passage**

SWIMMING POOL/HEALTH CLUB: **Yes**
CONFERENCE FACILITIES: **Up to 70**
PRICE GUIDE:
SINGLE: **£50/£85**
DOUBLE: **£100/170 (incl Dinner)**

Lea Hill Hotel

Membury, Axminster, East Devon EX13 7AQ
Tel: 040488 388

If you want to get away from it all, this could well be for you. A thatched Devon long-house with flag stoned floors, beams and inglenook fireplaces, Lea Hill has recently been acquired by Mr & Mrs Banks. With a considerable previous reputation for the quality of her cooking, Mrs Banks is in charge of the kitchen from whence comes delicious food served in the charmingly heavily beamed restaurant. Cosy bedrooms are in keeping with the character of the house. Here deep in the lush Devonshire countryside relax from the pressures of the outside world.

OPEN: **March to January 3rd**
NO. ROOMS: **14** EN SUITE **14**
ROOM TELEPHONES: **Yes** TV IN ROOMS: **Yes**
PETS: **Yes** CHILDREN: **Over 10**
DISABLED: **Unsuitable**

SWIMMING POOL/HEALTH CLUB: **No**
CONFERENCE FACILITIES: **No**
PRICE GUIDE:
SINGLE: **£60/£100** DOUBLE: **£80/£120**

Periton Park

Middlecombe, Nr Minehead, W. Somerset TA24 8SW
Tel: 0643 706885 · Fax: 0643 702698

Unspoilt is an overworked adjective beloved by Estate Agents, but it truly applies to the setting of this attractive Country House Hotel, from which you can walk directly away into, Yes, "unspoilt" country. Inside, pleasingly proportioned rooms are restful and tastefully furnished. Owners Richard and Angela Hunt take a personal interest in the welfare of their guests. In the appealing Dining Room you may sample excellent food and fine wines, following which you are assured of a comfortable bed. A great place for doing absolutely nothing ... in comfort!

OPEN: **March to January inclusive**	SWIMMING POOL/HEALTH CLUB:
NO. ROOMS: **8** EN SUITE **8**	**No**
ROOM TELEPHONES: **Yes** TV IN ROOMS: **Yes**	CONFERENCE FACILITIES:
PETS: **By arrangement** CHILDREN: **Over 12**	**Small Business Meetings**
DISABLED: **Yes**	PRICE GUIDE: SINGLE: **£80**
LOCATION: **Off A39 Minehead – Porlock road**	DOUBLE: **£120 (incl Dinner)**

The Kings Arms Inn

Montacute, Somerset TA16 6UU
Tel: 0935 822513 · Fax: 0935 826549

Close to the famous Elizabethan Montacute House, lies this pretty 16th century Inn. Considerable upgrading over the years has resulted in a most appealing place to stay or visit for a meal. All bedrooms, including a 4-poster are well furnished and appointed in keeping with the atmosphere of this character property. There is a charming lounge with exposed stone walls, whilst cuisine ranges from the popular Hot & Cold Buffet served at lunch times in the Pickwick Bar to more exotic fare for dinner presented in the elegant surroundings of the Abbey Room.

OPEN: *All year*
NO. ROOMS: *11* EN SUITE *11*
ROOM TELEPHONES: *Yes* TV IN ROOMS: *Yes*
PETS: *No* CHILDREN: *Yes*
DISABLED: *Unsuitable*

SWIMMING POOL/HEALTH CLUB: *No*
CONFERENCE FACILITIES: *No*
PRICE GUIDE:
SINGLE: *£42* DOUBLE: *£64*

Polurrian Hotel

Mullion, Lizard Peninsula, S. Cornwall TR12 7EN
Tel: 0326 240421 · Fax: 0326 240083

This impressive Edwardian building stands in a dramatic situation 300 feet above Polurrian Cove. Owned and operated for 45 years by the Francis family, the hotel offers the complete holiday for all the family. You dine by candle-light on tables laid with crystal and silver in a Dining Room with stunning views of Mounts Bay below, the accent being on sea fresh fish and organic vegetables and salads from the hotel's own garden. There is a superb new Leisure Club and when you are tired out a restful night is assured in a comfortable bed. Surrounded by spectacular National Trust coastline and cliffs, the Polurrian is the family hotel par excellence.

OPEN: **March to November**
NO. ROOMS: **40** EN SUITE **40**
ROOM TELEPHONES: **Yes** TV IN ROOMS: **Yes**
PETS: **Yes** CHILDREN: **Yes**
DISABLED: **Yes**

SWIMMING POOL/HEALTH CLUB:
Indoor/Outdoor
CONFERENCE FACILITIES: **In off season**
PRICE GUIDE: SINGLE: **£50/£78**
DOUBLE: **£126/£200 (inc Dinner)**

LOCATION: **Follow signs for Mullion Cove & look for hotel sign on right ½ mile from village**

Hollington House

Woolton Hill, Nr Newbury, Berkshire
Tel: 0635 255100 · Fax: 0635 255075

In 1992 this magnificent Edwardian Mansion was totally refurbished by resident owner John Guy and transformed into one of the finest hotels in this part of England. Period features abound, from the superb galleried oak panelled reception hall, to the delightful bedrooms, each individually designed with excellent bathrooms. Prior to opening Hollington House, John Guy operated one of the leading hotels in Australia. His chef, who has come with him, produces original and innovative dishes. There is a relaxed and congenial air here ... grand but not stuffy.

OPEN: **All year**
NO. ROOMS: **20** EN SUITE **20**
ROOM TELEPHONES: **Yes** TV IN ROOMS: **Yes**
PETS: **No** CHILDREN: **Yes** DISABLED: **Yes**
LOCATION: **From Newbury take A343 towards Andover, turn right for Woolton Hill, and then follow Herb Garden Signs**

SWIMMING POOL: **Outdoor Heated**
CONFERENCE FACILITIES:
Small Business Meetings up to 40
PRICE GUIDE:
SINGLE: **From £80** DOUBLE: **£105/£190**

Lakeside Hotel

Newby Bridge, Cumbria LA12 8AT
Tel: 05395 31207 · Fax: 05395 31699

Situated right on the edge of Lake Windermere as its name suggests, this fine traditional Lakeland hotel has been the subject of complete re-furbishment. Bedrooms have been individually designed, most having lake views. In an atmosphere of old beams, original panelling and lake shore terraces you can marvel at the beauty of this glorious area. Two restaurants feature menus based largely on fresh produce and Cumbrian specialities. Wherever your interests lie, the Lakeside makes a perfect base to come back to at the day's end.

OPEN: *All year*
NO. ROOMS: **69** EN SUITE **69**
ROOM TELEPHONES: *Yes* TV IN ROOMS: *Yes*
PETS: *Yes* CHILDREN: *Yes*
DISABLED: *Yes*
LOCATION: *From Newby Bridge turn right over bridge. Hotel is one mile on right*

SWIMMING POOL/HEALTH CLUB: *No*
CONFERENCE FACILITIES:
Up to 100 Theatre Style
PRICE GUIDE:
SINGLE: *£55/£85* DOUBLE: *£90/£140*

Passage House Hotel

Kingsteignton, Newton Abbot, Devon TQ12 3QH
Tel: 0626 55515 · Fax: 0626 63336

In a tranquil setting on the banks of the Teign looking down the estuary across placid waters, sits this fine hotel. Modern in design, interiors are co-ordinated in cool colours taking the mood of the surrounding countryside. Visitors will appreciate the easy access sited as it is on the edge of Torbay. With its superb Leisure Club, thoughtfully designed bedrooms, fine restaurant and every possible facility for the businessman, the Passage House combines the best of both worlds ... comfort and convenience.

OPEN: **All year**
NO. ROOMS: **39** EN SUITE **39**
ROOM TELEPHONES: **Yes** TV IN ROOMS: **Yes**
PETS: **By arrangement** CHILDREN: **Yes**
DISABLED: **Unsuitable**

SWIMMING POOL/HEALTH CLUB: **Yes**
CONFERENCE FACILITIES:
Business Meetings up to 100
PRICE GUIDE:
SINGLE: **£59/£65** DOUBLE: **£85/£100**

LOCATION: **Follow race course signs from A381 and turn left at mini-roundabout**

Ryedale Lodge

Nunnington, Nr Helmsley, York YO6 5XB
Tel: 04395 246

"Peace, tranquillity and good living" is the legend on the hotel's brochure. Owners Jon and Janet Laird ensure the "good living". The idyllic setting ensures the rest. This enchanting former railway station has charming individually styled bedrooms, some with spa baths, an elegant Lounge with deep soft chairs and sofas and a lovely Dining Room in which to enjoy Janet Laird's innovative cooking. It's no good waiting for the 4.30 from Paddington, the trains are now more ghosts but the "good living" steams on!

OPEN: **All year**
NO. ROOMS: **7** EN SUITE **7**
ROOM TELEPHONES: **Yes** TV IN ROOMS: **Yes**
PETS: **No** CHILDREN: **Yes**
DISABLED: **Unsuitable**
LOCATION: **Off B1257 Helmsley – Malton road**

SWIMMING POOL/HEALTH CLUB: **No**
CONFERENCE FACILITIES:
Small Business Meetings up to 25
PRICE GUIDE: SINGLE: **£82/£95 (incl Dinner)**
DOUBLE: **£135/£150 (incl Dinner)**

The Whipper-In Hotel

The Market Place, Oakham, Rutland LE15 6DT
Tel: 0572 756971 · Fax: 0572 757759

A highly individual 17th century coaching Inn of charm and character. With its beamed ceilings, old prints, fresh flower arrangements and antiques, the Whipper-In cossetts guests in the authentic atmosphere of a bygone era. Individually designed bedrooms, some with 4-posters, are extremely comfortable and have good bathrooms. Creative cooking, including home baking, is served in the delightful restaurant with its huge fireplace and beamed ceilings. Two intimate conference rooms offer comprehensive facilities for business meetings.

OPEN: ***All year***
NO. ROOMS: **25** EN SUITE **25**
ROOM TELEPHONES: **Yes** TV IN ROOMS: **Yes**
PETS: **Yes** CHILDREN: **Yes**
DISABLED: **Yes**

SWIMMING POOL/HEALTH CLUB: **No**
CONFERENCE FACILITIES:
Up to 50 Theatre Style
PRICE GUIDE: SINGLE: **£76.37 (Room only)**
DOUBLE: **£94 (Room only)**

The Hautboy

Ockham, Surrey GU23 6NP
Tel: 0483 225355 · Fax: 0483 211176

Every bit as unusual as its name suggests. The Hautboy takes its title from the note produced by the Oboe and its architectural origins are 19th century Victorian Gothic. Owners, Ian and Piera Shier have created five highly distinctive bedrooms with antiques, spa baths, good beds, even to a Victorian bathtub in the Byron Suite. The atmospheric restaurant serves interesting dishes from frequently changing menus, whilst the original Great Hall with Minstrels Gallery is the setting for the Brasserie where you can enjoy simpler fare. Truly one of Surreys most singular hotels.

OPEN: *All year*
NO. ROOMS: *5* EN SUITE *5*
ROOM TELEPHONES: *Yes* TV IN ROOMS: *Yes*
PETS: *No* CHILDREN: *By arrangement*
DISABLED: *Unsuitable*

SWIMMING POOL/HEALTH CLUB: *No*
CONFERENCE FACILITIES:
Business Meetings up to 40
PRICE GUIDE:
SINGLE: *£78* DOUBLE: *£98*

Otley House

Otley, Nr Ipswich, Suffolk IP6 9NR
Tel: 0473 890 253

Dating from the 17th century, Otley House stands in picturesque grounds complete with lake, ducks and moorhens. It is the home of Michael Hilton and his Danish wife Lise, who is responsible for the delicious Scandanavian and English fare. The elegant interiors are beautifully furnished and reflect the good taste of the owners. Interesting features include a Tudor fireplace, fine Georgian staircase, billiard room, and grand piano for those musically inclined. With its lovely well appointed bedrooms, Otley House is an individual retreat from which to escape the world.

OPEN: *1st March – 1st November*
NO. ROOMS: *4* EN SUITE *4*
ROOM TELEPHONES: *Avail* TV IN ROOMS: *Yes*
PETS: *Yes* CHILDREN: *Over 12*
DISABLED: *Yes*

SWIMMING POOL/HEALTH CLUB: *No*
CONFERENCE FACILITIES: *No*
PRICE GUIDE: SINGLE: *£53.50 (inc Dinner)*
DOUBLE: *£79 (incl Dinner)*

Redcliffe Hotel

Marine Drive, Paignton, Devon TQ3 2NL
Tel: 0803 526397

You wouldn't need the strength of a shot putter to reach the sea with a stone from this impressive hotel. Right on the waters edge of this bustling resort, the hotel offers comfortable well appointed bedrooms, elegant lounges and a restaurant where you can enjoy fine food and wines whilst admiring the panorama outside. This encompasses Tor Bay, taking in the Regency town of Torquay and across to the historic fishing port of Brixham. With its own ballroom and comprehensive leisure activities, this historic hotel is not only ideal for family holidays, but caters for conferences off season.

OPEN: **All year**
NO. ROOMS: **60** EN SUITE **60**
ROOM TELEPHONES: **Yes** TV IN ROOMS: **Yes**
PETS: **No** CHILDREN: **Yes**
DISABLED: **Unsuitable**

SWIMMING POOL: **Outdoor Heated**
CONFERENCE FACILITIES:
Business Meetings up to 100-150
PRICE GUIDE:
SINGLE: **£40/£50** DOUBLE: **£80/£100**

Jubilee Inn

Pelynt, Nr Looe, Cornwall PL13 2JZ
Tel: 0503 220312 · Fax: 0503 220920

This famous 15th century Inn is owned and operated by Tim & Judith Williams. The period atmosphere is apparent as soon as you enter the Inn, with its oak beams, great fireplaces with gleaming copper hoods, antique pieces, Delabole slate floors in the bar and fresh flowers in summer. In the charming restaurant emphasis is on fresh sea food caught locally at Looe, whilst real ale and an extensive selection of bar snacks is available in the bars. An unusual spiral staircase ascends to the bedrooms, designed by local artist Stuart Armfield, some of whose paintings adorn the walls.

OPEN: **All year**
NO. ROOMS: **12** EN SUITE **12**
ROOM TELEPHONES: **Yes** TV IN ROOMS: **Yes**
PETS: **Yes** CHILDREN: **Yes**
DISABLED: **Unsuitable**
LOCATION:

SWIMMING POOL/HEALTH CLUB: **No**
CONFERENCE FACILITIES: **No**
PRICE GUIDE:
SINGLE: **£33**
DOUBLE: **£56**

Temple Sowerby House Hotel

Temple Sowerby, Nr Penrith, Cumbria CA10 1RZ
Tel: 07683 61578 · Fax: 07683 61958

A particularly friendly and welcoming atmosphere exists at this old Cumbrian house owned and operated by Anne and Peter McNamara. The hotel is situated in 2 acres of grounds including a lovely walled garden overlooking Cross Fell, highest of the Pennine Peaks. Comfortable bedrooms, a cosy lounge and panelled dining room serving good food typify Temple Sowerby House, which is ideally located just 5 miles from the motorway network in the unspoilt Eden Valley.

OPEN: **All year**
NO. ROOMS: **12** EN SUITE **12**
ROOM TELEPHONES: **Yes** TV IN ROOMS: **Yes**
PETS: **Yes** CHILDREN: **Yes**
DISABLED: **Yes**
LOCATION: **Off A66 5 miles from Jcn 40 on M6**

SWIMMING POOL/HEALTH CLUB: **No**
CONFERENCE FACILITIES:
Small Business Meetings up to 12
PRICE GUIDE:
SINGLE: **£45/£50** DOUBLE: **£56/£70**

Orton Hall Hotel

The Village, Orton Longueville, Peterborough, Cambridgeshire PE2 7DN
Tel: 0733 391111 · Fax: 0733 231912

This impressive 17th century mansion is being painstakingly restored to enable todays guests to sample for a while, life in the "grand" manner. Each bedroom has its own character, some with 4-posters and others designated for non-smokers. Good food can be sampled in the mellow ambience of the oak panelled Huntly Restaurant whilst in the Conservatory with its 16th century teracotta floors and stained glass, take tea and soak up the tranquillity. In boardrooms, syndicate rooms and the Great Room, every possible high tech facility is provided to ensure the success of your conference.

OPEN: ***All year***
NO. ROOMS: **50** EN SUITE **50**
ROOM TELEPHONES: **Yes** TV IN ROOMS: **Yes**
PETS: **Yes** CHILDREN: **Yes**
DISABLED: **Yes**

SWIMMING POOL/HEALTH CLUB:
Not until '94
CONFERENCE FACILITIES: **Yes**
PRICE GUIDE:
SINGLE: **£76.65** DOUBLE: **£103.65**

The Mansion House

Thames Street, Poole, Dorset BH15 1JN
Tel: 0202 685666 · Fax: 0202 665709

Not merely a hotel, but a Dining Club as well with 3,000 members, which affords discounts on accommodation, food and wine. A brigade of talented chefs present a vast variety of inventive dishes, classical, traditional and modern. Bedrooms are particularly pleasing with fresh modern decor, quality furnishings and excellent bathrooms. From the elegant staircase flanked by pillars to the graceful private rooms for dining and meetings, this fetching Georgian house in its quiet backwater should suit the more discerning guest.

OPEN: **All year**
NO. ROOMS: **28** EN SUITE **28**
ROOM TELEPHONES: **Yes** TV IN ROOMS: **Yes**
PETS: **No** CHILDREN: **Yes**
DISABLED: **Unsuitable**
LOCATION: **Off the Quay**

SWIMMING POOL/HEALTH CLUB: **No**
CONFERENCE FACILITIES:
Small Business Meetings up to 30
PRICE GUIDE:
SINGLE: **£79/£85** DOUBLE: **£100/£120**

The Oaks Hotel

Porlock, West Somerset TA24 8ES
Tel: 0643 862265

This charming Edwardian Country House is run in very friendly fashion by owners Tim and Anne Riley. There is a genuine warmth of welcome which matches the crackling log fires that burn in inclement weather. From the elegant well proportioned Drawing Room to the cosy Cocktail Bar to the delightful Dining Room, this small hotel has great appeal. Food is truly excellent, varied and interesting. Menus change daily. Bedrooms are immaculately maintained with good bathrooms. Surrounded by glorious coast and country, The Oaks is marvellous value for money ... a positive bargain.

OPEN: **All year**
NO. ROOMS: **11** EN SUITE **11**
ROOM TELEPHONES: **Yes** TV IN ROOMS: **Yes**
PETS: **Yes** CHILDREN: **Yes**
DISABLED: **Unsuitable**
LOCATION: **Off A39 on entering village**

SWIMMING POOL/HEALTH CLUB:
No
CONFERENCE FACILITIES: **No**
PRICE GUIDE: SINGLE: **£65**
DOUBLE: **£110 (incl Dinner)**

Port Gaverne Hotel

Port Gaverne, Nr Port Isaac, N. Cornwall PL29 3SQ
Tel: 0208 880244 · Fax: 0208 880151

A genuine 17th century Inn combining the character and atmosphere of a bygone era with 20th century amenities. Owned since 1969 by Fred and Midge Ross, the hotel nestles in a sheltered cove and dispenses hospitality to all and sundry. Bedrooms are cosy with many extras. Lining the walls is a unique collection of old photographs, oils and watercolours depicting many of the wrecks which have foundered on this wild coast. A wide variety of food is served in the Dining Room and Bars and features local specialities. Surrounded by National Trust land Port Gaverne makes an ideal retreat from the modern world.

OPEN: *February 22nd to January 12th*
NO. ROOMS: *19* EN SUITE *19*
ROOM TELEPHONES: *Yes* TV IN ROOMS: *Yes*
PETS: *Yes* CHILDREN: *Yes*
DISABLED: *Unsuitable*
LOCATION: *Signposted from B3314 south of Delabole via B3267*

SWIMMING POOL/HEALTH CLUB: *No*
CONFERENCE FACILITIES: *No*
PRICE GUIDE:
SINGLE: *£40/44* DOUBLE: *£80/£88*

The Lugger Hotel

Portloe, Nr Truro, Cornwall TR2 5RD
Tel: 0872 501322 · Fax: 0872 501691

Perhaps everyone's idea of romantic Cornwall: a picturesque cove surrounded by rugged cliffs and hanging over the water a 17th century Inn. Echoes of its smuggling past can be felt in the oak beamed lounge with Cornish stone fireplace and the tiny Cocktail Bar which together with the Dining Room look right down on the cove. This atmospheric small hotel is owned and run by the Powell family and has to be one of the prettiest in Cornwall. Cosy bedrooms with every facility, good food, fine wines (even Cornish wine!) and friendly hosts add up to an unbeatable combination.

OPEN: ***Early February to end November***
NO. ROOMS: ***19*** EN SUITE ***19***
ROOM TELEPHONES: ***Yes*** TV IN ROOMS: ***Yes***
PETS: ***No*** CHILDREN: ***Over 12***
DISABLED: ***Unsuitable***
LOCATION: ***Take A3078 from Tregony***

SWIMMING POOL/HEALTH CLUB: ***No***
CONFERENCE FACILITIES: ***No***
PRICE GUIDE:
SINGLE: ***£45/£65 (incl Dinner)***
DOUBLE: ***£90/£130 (incl Dinner)***

Chequers Hotel

Church Place, Pulborough, West Sussex RH20 1AD
Tel: 0798 872486 · Fax: 0798 872715

This charming small Grade 2 listed hotel is owned and operated by the very welcoming Searancke family, who go out of their way to ensure the phrase "personal attention" is no mere cliche. Immaculate housekeeping standards and value for money are big plus points, as are the pretty bedrooms with their many thoughtful extras, the excellent food, and the delightful Conservatory Coffee Shop. Overlooking the Arun Valley and at the very heart of Sussex, Chequers is ideal for those seeking concerned personal service.

OPEN: **All year**
NO. ROOMS: **11** EN SUITE **10**
ROOM TELEPHONES: **Yes** TV IN ROOMS: **Yes**
PETS: **Yes** CHILDREN: **Yes**
DISABLED: **Unsuitable**
LOCATION: **Just off main A29 onto Bridlepath**

SWIMMING POOL/HEALTH CLUB: **No**
CONFERENCE FACILITIES:
Small Business Meetings up to 28
PRICE GUIDE: SINGLE: **£47.50/£50**
DOUBLE: **£75/£85**

The Pear Tree at Purton

Church End, Purton, Swindon, Wiltshire SN5 9ED
Tel: 0793 772100 · Fax: 0793 772369

If the former incumbent of this old Vicarage were to return today, he would probably do a double take! Owners Francis and Anne Young have worked a remarkable transformation in just a few years. The entire hotel is artistically designed and beautifully furnished. Justifiably, the fascinating Conservatory Restaurant has won many accolades for its cuisine whilst the outlook across the colourful Victorian garden is as delectable as the food. With its fresh flower arrangements and one of the tallest Weeping Figs I have seen. The Pear Tree is as charming as its name suggests.

OPEN: **All year**
NO. ROOMS: **18** EN SUITE **18**
ROOM TELEPHONES: **Yes** TV IN ROOMS: **Yes**
PETS: **By arrangement** CHILDREN: **Yes**
DISABLED: **Yes**
LOCATION: **In Purton turn right at Lloyds Bank**

SWIMMING POOL/HEALTH CLUB: **No**
CONFERENCE FACILITIES:
Small Business Meetings up to 30
PRICE GUIDE:
SINGLE: **£87** DOUBLE: **£87/£97**

The Burgoyne Hotel

Reeth, Richmond, N. Yorks DL11 6SN
Tel: 0748 84292 · Fax: 0748 84691

If there is better value for money than this anywhere in Yorkshire, then I don't know it. Extremely hospitable owners, Peter Cawardine and Derek Hichson have created an oasis of good living in this unspoilt village in the heart of Swaledale, famous as the mid-point on Wainwrights Coast to Coast walk. Superb food, comfortable bedrooms, a most appealing Dining Room and lovely Drawing Room with log fire, many hotels can also claim the same, but not all have that warmth of atmosphere that makes The Burgoyne that little bit special.

OPEN: **All year**
NO. ROOMS: **8** EN SUITE **8**
ROOM TELEPHONES: **No** TV IN ROOMS: **Yes**
PETS: **By arrangement** CHILDREN: **Yes**
DISABLED: **Unsuitable**
LOCATION: **On the Green at Reeth**

SWIMMING POOL/HEALTH CLUB:
No
CONFERENCE FACILITIES:
Small Business Meetings up to 8
PRICE GUIDE: SINGLE: **£55** DOUBLE: **£65**

The Brookhouse

Rolleston-on-Dove, Nr Burton-on-Trent, Staffordshire
Tel: 0283 814188 · Fax: 0283 813644

This creeper clad William and Mary Grade 2 listed building is situated in a tranquil brookside backwater and is owned by welcoming John Westwood. The bedrooms are particularly interesting with a collection of superb antique beds, 4-posters, half testers and Victorian brass beds, some dressed with Nottingham lace. In the beamed Restaurant candle-light and fresh flowers adorn tables laid with silver and crystal. A relaxed atmosphere in which to enjoy really delicious food and fine wines.

OPEN: ***All year***
NO. ROOMS: ***19*** EN SUITE ***19***
ROOM TELEPHONES: ***Yes*** TV IN ROOMS: ***Yes***
PETS: ***Yes*** CHILDREN: ***Over 12***
DISABLED: ***Yes***
LOCATION: ***Hotel lies between A50 and A38***

SWIMMING POOL/HEALTH CLUB: ***No***
CONFERENCE FACILITIES:
Small Business Meetings up to 16
PRICE GUIDE:
SINGLE: ***£65/£75*** DOUBLE: ***£79/£89***

The Rose and Crown Hotel

Romaldkirk, Barnard Castle, Co Durham DL12 9EB
Tel: 0833 50213 · Fax: 0833 50828

The kind of "horse power" may be slightly different to that which brought travellers to this Inn in 1733, but hospitality is still being dispensed as it was then in an atmosphere of copper, brass and log fires. Food is of particular importance at the Rose & Crown. Owners Christopher and Alison Davy present traditional English fare with local produce forming the basis of daily changing menus. There is much to see and do in unspoilt Teesdale. An interesting colony of bats make their home at Romaldkirk, who knows, you might even see one?

OPEN: *All year*
NO. ROOMS: *13* EN SUITE *13*
ROOM TELEPHONES: *Yes* TV IN ROOMS: *Yes*
PETS: *Yes* CHILDREN: *Yes*
DISABLED: *Yes*
LOCATION: *6 miles N.W. of Barnard Castle on B6277*

SWIMMING POOL/HEALTH CLUB: *No*
CONFERENCE FACILITIES:
None
PRICE GUIDE:
SINGLE: *£50* DOUBLE: *£75*

Pengethley Manor

Nr Ross-on-Wye, Herefordshire HR9 6LL
Tel: 098987 211 · Fax: 098987 238

This former country squire's house is set in 15 acres of well manicured gardens and grounds complete with trout lake. The hotel offers a considerable variety of bedrooms from the Titled rooms in the Manor with their period atmosphere, to those in the Courtyard which have their individual character. Local produce and herbs from the garden form the basis of succulent food for which the hotel is noted. Breakfasts are excellent and feature free range eggs. Conferences in the Chandos Conference Centre have every possible facility.

OPEN: **All year**
NO. ROOMS: **24** EN SUITE **24**
ROOM TELEPHONES: **Yes** TV IN ROOMS: **Yes**
PETS: **Yes** CHILDREN: **Yes**
DISABLED: **Yes**
LOCATION: **5 miles from Ross-on-Wye on A49 towards Hereford**

SWIMMING POOL: **Outdoor Heated**
CONFERENCE FACILITIES:
Business Meetings up to 80
PRICE GUIDE:
SINGLE: **£70/£115** DOUBLE: **£100/£154**

Stone House

Rushlake Green, Heathfield, East Sussex TN21 9QJ
Tel: 0435 830553 · Fax: 0435 830726

Peter and Jane Dunn extend a warm welcome to their beautiful Manor House. Of great architectural interest, the charming rooms have been sympathetically restored and very much convey the air of a "home" (which indeed it is) rather than an hotel. 20th century conveniences blend well with antiques, fine fabrics, old English china, silver and embroidery. Since the Dunns only cater for residents, peace and un-disturbed tranquillity is assured in an atmosphere of woods, fields, log fires, croquet and fresh food from the estate.

OPEN: **All year except 1 month from Dec 24th**
NO. ROOMS: **8** EN SUITE **7**
ROOM TELEPHONES: **Yes** TV IN ROOMS: **Yes**
PETS: **Yes** CHILDREN: **Over 9**
DISABLED: **Unsuitable**

SWIMMING POOL/HEALTH CLUB: **No**
CONFERENCE FACILITIES:
Small Business Meetings up to 16
PRICE GUIDE: SINGLE: **£50/£71.25**

Bolt Head Hotel

Sharpitor, Salcombe, S. Devon TQ8 8LL
Tel: 054884 3751 · Fax: 054884 3060

Spectacular is no exaggeration when applied to the panoramic marine views from this Norwegian designed hotel perched above the glittering blue waters of the Salcombe Estuary. Colourful furnishings greet you on arrival in the reception Lounge. Bedrooms are well appointed, a combination of pine furniture and Laura Ashley fabrics, most have sea views. From the split level Dining Room the same sensational views of the coastline are obtained. Colourful umbrellas, sun balconies and a Swimming Pool all convey a Continental air.

OPEN: *April 1st to mid-November*
NO. ROOMS: *28* EN SUITE *28*
ROOM TELEPHONES: *Yes* TV IN ROOMS: *Yes*
PETS: *Yes* CHILDREN: *Yes*
DISABLED: *Unsuitable*
LOCATION: *Take coast road signposted South Sands*

SWIMMING POOL: *Outdoor*
CONFERENCE FACILITIES: *No*
PRICE GUIDE:
SINGLE: *From £59*
DOUBLE: *£118 (incl Dinner)*

Wrea Head Country Hotel

Scalby, Nr Scarborough, North Yorkshire YO13 0PB
Tel: 0723 378211 · Fax: 0723 371780

A continuous programme of upgrading has turned this former Victorian house into one of the most luxurious and individual hotels in North Yorkshire. Impressively proportioned rooms have a wealth of fine panelling, antiques, original paintings and log fires. Captivating bedrooms are beautifully furnished whilst in the distinctive atmosphere of the Russell Flint Restaurant (so-called because of the famous water-colourist's works which adorn the walls) cooking in the best traditions of the English country house can be enjoyed.

OPEN: **All year**
NO. ROOMS: **21** EN SUITE **21**
ROOM TELEPHONES: **Yes** TV IN ROOMS: **Yes**
PETS: **By arrangement** CHILDREN: **Yes**
DISABLED: **Yes**

SWIMMING POOL/HEALTH CLUB: **No**
CONFERENCE FACILITIES:
Small Business Meetings up to 21
PRICE GUIDE:
SINGLE: **£45/£60** DOUBLE: **£90/£120**

Holbeck Hall Hotel

Seacliff Road, South Cliff, Scarborough, N. Yorkshire YO11 2XX
Tel: 0723 374374 · Fax: 0723 351114

This imposing Victorian Mansion sits in its own delightful grounds commanding a superb panorama of coast and country. From the majestic Baronial Hall with its great fireplace and Minstrels Gallery, an elegant staircase ascends to the pleasing bedrooms. Quality furnishings are complemented by fine crystal and soft lighting in the classic Rose Lounge. Of interest to film buffs is the fact that Holbeck Hall was once owned by the family of the famous actor Charles Laughton.

OPEN: *All year*
NO. ROOMS: *30* EN SUITE *30*
ROOM TELEPHONES: *Yes* TV IN ROOMS: *Yes*
PETS: *No* CHILDREN: *Yes*
DISABLED: *Unsuitable*

SWIMMING POOL/HEALTH CLUB: *No*
CONFERENCE FACILITIES:
Small Business Meetings up to 30
PRICE GUIDE:
SINGLE: *£55/£75* DOUBLE: *£110/£150*

The Royal Oak

High Street, Sevenoaks, Kent TN13 1HY
Tel: 0732 451109 · Fax: 0732 740187

Easy access from Motorways M25, M20 and M26 make this 17th century hotel an ideal base for visiting London and the "Garden of England". Total re-furbishment has resulted in a most appealing atmosphere. In the intimate and elegant surroundings of the restaurant, local Kentish produce forms the basis of unusual dishes, a combination of nouvelle cuisines and traditional English fare. With its stylish conservatory, delightful bedrooms and well equipped conference rooms, The Royal Oak continues to dispense hospitality as it has done for hundreds of years.

OPEN: *All year*
NO. ROOMS: *39* EN SUITE *39*
ROOM TELEPHONES: *Yes* TV IN ROOMS: *Yes*
PETS: *No* CHILDREN: *Yes*
DISABLED: *Yes*

SWIMMING POOL/HEALTH CLUB: *No*
CONFERENCE FACILITIES:
Up to 30 Theatre Style
PRICE GUIDE: SINGLE: *£70.50 (Room only)*
DOUBLE: *£94 (Room only)*

The Charnwood Hotel

10, Sharrow Lane, Sheffield, Yorks S11 8AA
Tel: 0742 589411 · Fax: 0742 555107

It comes as something of a shock to find such an elegant hotel as this in the environs of a major city. You have a choice of two Restaurants: Henfreys, all charm and elegance with its graceful proportions, lace table cloths, unique fireplace and baby grand piano, or Brasserie Leo with its stunningly imaginative decor. Individual bedrooms are exceptionally comfortable with lovely bathrooms. This captivating Georgian Mansion offers unusual standards of comfort.

OPEN: *All year*
NO. ROOMS: *22* EN SUITE *22*
ROOM TELEPHONES: *Yes* TV IN ROOMS: *Yes*
PETS: *No* CHILDREN: *Yes*
DISABLED: *Unsuitable*
LOCATION: *Off Sheffield – Chesterfield road*

SWIMMING POOL/HEALTH CLUB: *No*
CONFERENCE FACILITIES:
Theatre Style up to 80
PRICE GUIDE:
SINGLE: *£78* DOUBLE: *£95*

The Eastbury

Long Street, Sherborne, Dorset DT9 3BY
Tel: 0935 813131 · Fax: 0935 817296

"Standards you had forgotten existed" is the promise on the brochure of this elegant hotel in the heart of romantic Thomas Hardy country. This enchanting town-house has recently been sympathetically restored retaining much of the original character, even to a library of antiquarian books. The intimate atmosphere of a fine country house which prevails at The Eastbury is perhaps only possible in a small establishment where each guest receives concerned personal service. The three "C's" very much apply here ... Cuisine, Comfort and Care!

OPEN: **All year**
NO. ROOMS: **15** EN SUITE **15**
ROOM TELEPHONES: **Yes** TV IN ROOMS: **Yes**
PETS: **No** CHILDREN: **Yes**
DISABLED: **Unsuitable**

SWIMMING POOL/HEALTH CLUB: **No**
CONFERENCE FACILITIES:
Business Meetings up to 80
PRICE GUIDE:
SINGLE: **£72.50** DOUBLE: **£98**

Daneswood House Hotel

Cuck Hill, Shipham, Nr Bristol, Somerset BS25 1RD
Tel: 093484 3145 · Fax: 093484 3824

This former Edwardian Health Hydro lies in a magnificent position with superb panoramic views as far as S. Wales and the Brecon Beacons. Relaxed informality in an atmosphere of period elegance has been achieved by resident owners, David & Elise Hodges. Each of the bedrooms have been furnished with flair and include a king sized bed in the honeymoon suite to garden suites with gallery bedrooms and whirlpool baths. Cuisine is English and French with unusual dishes presented in the elegant dining room. Full conference facilities are available with comprehensive back up equipment as required.

OPEN: **All year**
NO. ROOMS: **12 EN SUITE 12**
ROOM TELEPHONES: **Yes** TV IN ROOMS: **Yes**
PETS: **By arrangement**
CHILDREN: **By arrangement** DISABLED: **Yes**
LOCATION: **Off A38 12 miles south of Bristol**

SWIMMING POOL/HEALTH CLUB: **No**
CONFERENCE FACILITIES:
Small Business Meetings up to 25
PRICE GUIDE: SINGLE: **£57.50/£67.50**
DOUBLE: **£65/£112**

The Victoria Hotel

The Esplanade, Sidmouth, Devon EX10 8RY
Tel: 0395 512651 · Fax: 0395 579154

Echoes of a more gracious age are reflected in this rather "grand" hotel where old fashioned standards of service live on. Public rooms are impressively proportioned with many period features, comfortable furnishings and fresh flower arrangements. Most of the delightful bedrooms face South enjoying lovely coastal views, many have their own French windows and private balconies. Superb leisure facilities include a fabulous Spanish style pool, sauna, solarium, spa-bath and hair salon. I am sure Queen Victoria would have approved this elegant hotel that so proudly bears her name.

OPEN: **All year**
NO. ROOMS: **63** EN SUITE **63**
ROOM TELEPHONES: **Yes** TV IN ROOMS: **Yes**
PETS: **No** CHILDREN: **Yes**
DISABLED: **Unsuitable**

SWIMMING POOL: **Indoor and Outdoor**
CONFERENCE FACILITIES:
Business Meetings up to 60
PRICE GUIDE:
SINGLE: **From £78** DOUBLE: **From £145**

Simonsbath House Hotel

Simonsbath, Nr Minehead, Somerset TA24 7SH
Tel: 064383 259

You may think you have entered a time warp as you step into this delectable small hotel with it's mellow oak panelling, fresh flowers and log fires. Lovely bedrooms are tastefully appointed, some have 4-posters, and enjoy superb views of Exmoor. In the Dining Room, laid with fine porcelain and sparkling crystal, delicious home cooking is served. Here in the romantic country of Lorna Doone, the magic of more leisured days will capture your heart. Under the personal supervision of the owners, Mike and Sue Burns.

OPEN: **February 1st to November 30th**
NO. ROOMS: 7 EN SUITE 7
ROOM TELEPHONES: **Yes** TV IN ROOMS: **Yes**
PETS: **No** CHILDREN: **Welcome over 10**
DISABLED: **Unsuitable**
LOCATION: **On junction of B3223 and B3358 at Simonsbath**

SWIMMING POOL/HEALTH CLUB:
No
CONFERENCE FACILITIES:
No
PRICE GUIDE: SINGLE: **£50/£60** DOUBLE: **£90**

Singleton Lodge

Lodge Lane, Singleton, Nr Blackpool, Lancashire FY6 8LT
Tel: 0253 883854 · Fax: 0253 894432

This former Vicarage is situated in its own 5 acres of peaceful grounds and yet is a mere 15 minutes drive from the glittering attractions of the world famous resort of Blackpool. If a relaxed country house atmosphere operated by genuinely warm hearted owners is what you seek, Singleton Lodge should fit the bill. Alan and Ann Smith offer traditional English food and comfortable bedrooms at rates that don't require a meeting with your bank manager!

OPEN: **All year**
NO. ROOMS: **10** EN SUITE **10**
ROOM TELEPHONES: **Yes** TV IN ROOMS: **Yes**
PETS: **By arrangement** CHILDREN: **Yes**
DISABLED: **Unsuitable**

SWIMMING POOL/HEALTH CLUB: **No**
CONFERENCE FACILITIES: **Up to 12 or larger numbers by arrangement**
PRICE GUIDE:
SINGLE: **£45/£55** DOUBLE: **£65/£70**

LOCATION: **3 miles from Jcn 3 on M55 off A585 Fleetwood Rd, turn left at lights & left next lights**

Parrock Head Country Farmhouse Hotel

Slaidburn, Clitheroe, Lancs BB7 3AH
Tel: 02006 614

A perfect example of a 17th century farmhouse reposing in rural seclusion amidst unspoilt fells and valleys. Parrock Head is run in a very personal way by owners Richard and Vicky Umbers. You will be captivated by the snug bar, low beams, cosy bedrooms and the charming hay-loft lounge with its comfortable chairs, antique pieces, and fresh flower arrangements. Daily changing menus rely on fresh produce and home grown herbs to produce appetising dishes. Breakfasts are exceptional.

OPEN: **All year**
NO. ROOMS: **9** EN SUITE **9**
ROOM TELEPHONES: **Yes** TV IN ROOMS: **Yes**
PETS: **By arrangement** CHILDREN: **Yes**
DISABLED: **Yes**

SWIMMING POOL: **Outdoor Heated**
CONFERENCE FACILITIES:
Small Business Meetings up to 20
PRICE GUIDE:
SINGLE: **£35/£37.50** DOUBLE: **£56.50/£59**

LOCATION: **At Slaidburn take road With Hark to Bounty on your right, hotel is 1 mile on left**

Collaven Manor

Sourton, Devon EX20 4HH
Tel: 083786 522 · Fax: 083786 570

This small, picturesque 15th century Manor House is situated in a tranquil position on the edge of Dartmoor. The ambience here is informal and relaxed, in an atmosphere of oak beams, log fires and fresh flowers in Summer. Each of the comfortable bedrooms is individual in decor and design, whilst in the charming restaurant, you can enjoy good food and fine wines. Privately owned and operated by Katie Chappel, Collaven Manor is ideally placed for touring the whole of the West Country.

OPEN: **All year (except two weeks Dec/Jan)**
NO. ROOMS: **9** EN SUITE **9**
ROOM TELEPHONES: **Yes** TV IN ROOMS: **Yes**
PETS: **By arrangement** CHILDREN: **Yes**
DISABLED: **Unsuitable**
LOCATION: **Off A386 Okehampton – Tavistock road**

SWIMMING POOL/HEALTH CLUB: **No**
CONFERENCE FACILITIES:
Small Business Meetings up to 12
PRICE GUIDE:
SINGLE: **£51** DOUBLE: **£80/£95**

South Walsham Hall

South Walsham, Norfolk NR13 6DQ
Tel: 0605 49378

Beautiful grounds complete with a placid lake surround this elegant building whose origins date back to the Domesday Book. Ideally placed for visiting the world famous Norfolk Broads, South Walsham Hall offers todays visitor comfortable accommodation, including a particularly spacious bridal suite with luxury bathroom. Local specialities feature prominently on the extensive menus and there is an interesting wine list specially imported by the Swiss owners. The lovely grounds include a comprehensive Sport & Leisure Centre.

OPEN: **All year**
NO. ROOMS: **17** EN SUITE **17**
ROOM TELEPHONES: **Yes** TV IN ROOMS: **Yes**
PETS: **Yes** CHILDREN: **Yes**
DISABLED: **Yes**

SWIMMING POOL: **Outdoor Heated**
CONFERENCE FACILITIES:
Small Business Meetings up to 20
PRICE GUIDE:
SINGLE: **£40/£80** DOUBLE: **£50/£120**

Trevaunance Point Hotel

Trevaunance Cove, St Agnes, Cornwall TR5 0RZ
Tel: 0872 553235 · Fax: 0872 553874

Perched on the very edge of the cliffs above the ancient cove of Trevaunance is this old Cornish house, once the home of the famous film star Claude Rains and the setting for a Sherlock Holmes film. Owned and operated by Marc Watts, the atmosphere here is very relaxed and friendly. If you are looking for gold plated designer decor, this may not be for you, but if you want the flavour of old Cornwall, then this homely hotel with good food and seas crashing on the rocks below your bedroom window will recharge your mental batteries.

OPEN: **All year**
NO. ROOMS: **8** EN SUITE **8**
ROOM TELEPHONES: **Yes** TV IN ROOMS: **Yes**
PETS: **Yes** CHILDREN: **Yes**
DISABLED: **Unsuitable**

SWIMMING POOL/HEALTH CLUB: **No**
CONFERENCE FACILITIES:
Small Business Meetings up to 30
PRICE GUIDE:
SINGLE: **£40/£60** DOUBLE: **£60/£85**

The Carlyon Bay Hotel

St Austell, Cornwall PL25 8RD
Tel: 072681 2304 · Fax: 072681 4938

The Carlyon Bay and golf ... golf and the Carlyon Bay, the two are inseparable. Magnificently positioned in 250 acres of cliff land, this impressive establishment is undoubtedly one of the West Country's major hotels. Crystal chandeliers grace public areas and in the splendid restaurant you can choose from extensive menus whilst admiring the spectacular views. Excellent bedrooms vary from comfortable to de-luxe and are served by a lift. With its superb leisure complex, magnificent golf course and lovely gardens, there is something for everyone at The Carlyon Bay.

OPEN: **All year**
NO. ROOMS: **74** EN SUITE **74**
ROOM TELEPHONES: **Yes** TV IN ROOMS: **Yes**
PETS: **No** CHILDREN: **Yes**
DISABLED: **Yes**

SWIMMING POOL: **Indoor and Outdoor**
CONFERENCE FACILITIES:
Business Meetings up to 70
PRICE GUIDE:
SINGLE: **From £65** DOUBLE: **From £120**

Garrack Hotel

Burthallan Lane, St. Ives, Cornwall TR26 3AA
Tel: 0736 796199 · Fax: 0736 798955

Owned and operated by the welcoming Kilby family, this ivy clad hotel commands extensive views of the whole of St. Ives Bay, including the Island and Porthmeor Beach with its dramatic Atlantic rollers pounding on the shore. Families are particularly catered for with the hotel's small Leisure Centre which includes a heated Spa Pool, Whirlpool and Swim Jet, Sauna, Solarium and Leisure area where snacks are available. Many of the bedrooms have superb views whilst in the Restaurant you have a choice of table d'hote and a la carte menus backed by an interesting and reasonably priced wine list.

OPEN: ***All year***
NO. ROOMS: ***18*** EN SUITE ***18***
ROOM TELEPHONES: ***Yes*** TV IN ROOMS: ***Yes***
PETS: ***By prior arrangement*** CHILDREN: ***Yes***
DISABLED: ***Unsuitable***
LOCATION: ***From B3306 head for signs to Porthmeor Beach & look for hotel sign***

SWIMMING POOL/LEISURE CENTRE: ***Yes***
CONFERENCE FACILITIES:
Up to 25 Boardroom Style (off season)
PRICE GUIDE: SINGLE: ***£37.50/£49.50***
DOUBLE: ***£75/£99***

The Idle Rocks Hotel

St Mawes, Cornwall TR2 5AN
Tel: 0326 270771 · Fax: 0326 270062

It simply would not be possible to get closer to the water than this. You lie in bed and there is the sea sparkling below your window. Very continental in its atmosphere, The Idle Rocks has recently been the subject of a total transformation, turning it into one of the finest hotels in the delectable Duchy. Beautifully furnished with many antiques, the interiors are striking and elegant. Bedrooms are most appealing each one individual with superior bathrooms. Emphasis in the restaurant is on local sea food and the hotel even boasts its own bakery and patisserie. So here it is ... luxury and charm at the edge of the sea.

OPEN: **All year**
NO. ROOMS: **24** EN SUITE **24**
ROOM TELEPHONES: **Yes** TV IN ROOMS: **Yes**
PETS: **By arrangement** CHILDREN: **Yes**
DISABLED: **Yes**

SWIMMING POOL/HEALTH CLUB: **No**
CONFERENCE FACILITIES:
No
PRICE GUIDE:
SINGLE: **£25/£58** DOUBLE: **£50/£116**

Gabriel Court

Stoke Gabriel, Nr Totnes, S. Devon TQ9 6SF
Tel: 0803 782206 · Fax: 0803 782333

Dominated by a magnificent Magnolia tree, this old Manor House dating from 1487 is owned and run by Michael and Eryl Beacom. A friendly relaxed place with antiques and log fires in winter. Comfortable bedrooms, most South facing have views across the Elizabethan terraced gardens. Good English cooking is based on the hotel's own garden produce, with fish from the River Dart and sea food from Brixham. This pleasant hotel nestles in one of Devon's prettiest villages with its cobbles, orchards and bobbing boats.

OPEN: **March to January (inclusive)**
NO. ROOMS: **20** EN SUITE **20**
ROOM TELEPHONES: **Yes** TV IN ROOMS: **Yes**
PETS: **Yes** CHILDREN: **Yes**
DISABLED: **Unsuitable**
LOCATION: **One mile from Totnes. Turn right for Stoke Gabriel**

SWIMMING POOL: **Outdoor Heated**
CONFERENCE FACILITIES:
Small Business Meetings up to 20
PRICE GUIDE:
SINGLE: **£58** DOUBLE: **From £78**

Little Thakeham

Merrywood Lane, Storrington, West Sussex RH20 3HE
Tel: 0903 744416 · Fax: 0903 745022

Sir Edwin Lutyens created a small masterpiece with this exquisite Manor. Tim and Pauline Ractliffe have sympathetically converted it into one of Britain's finest country house hotels. The ambience is one of relaxed comfort in an atmosphere of log fires and antiques overlooked by a beautiful Minstrels Gallery. The bedroom suites are supremely comfortable each furnished in highly individual style. In the charming restaurant local produce forms the basis of the interesting dishes backed by an imaginative wine list. Little Thakeham is surrounded by magnificent gardens complementing the peace and tranquillity of the house.

OPEN: **All year**
NO. ROOMS: **9** EN SUITE **9**
ROOM TELEPHONES: **Yes** TV IN ROOMS: **Yes**
PETS: **No** CHILDREN: **Yes**
DISABLED: **Unsuitable**

SWIMMING POOL: **Outdoor Heated**
CONFERENCE FACILITIES:
Small Business Meetings up to 10
PRICE GUIDE:
SINGLE: **£95** DOUBLE: **£150**

LOCATION: **Off B2139 Storrington - Thakeham Rd 1 mile from Storrington turn right**

Abingworth Hall

Thakeham, Nr Storrington, West Sussex
Tel: 0798 813636 · Fax: 0798 813914

The one time home of Sir Oswald Mosley, this agreeable hotel, situated in its own peaceful 10 acre garden with ornamental lake conveys an atmosphere of repose. Owners Philip and Pauline Bulman have tried to re-create the ambience and style of the Hall's former days. Bedrooms are traditional in design whilst cuisine is based on fresh produce with home baking, even the preserves and ice-cream are home made. Only 25 miles from the M25 and M23 Motorways, and with two Heli-Pads. Abingworth is "worth" finding!

OPEN: **All year**
NO. ROOMS: **21** EN SUITE **21**
ROOM TELEPHONES: **Yes** TV IN ROOMS: **Yes**
PETS: **No** CHILDREN: **Over 10**
DISABLED: **By Arrangement**
LOCATION: **Off B2139 two miles from Storrington**

SWIMMING POOL: **Outdoor Heated**
CONFERENCE FACILITIES:
Small Business Meetings up to 24
PRICE GUIDE:
SINGLE: **£70** DOUBLE: **£96/£136**

Ettington Park

Alderminster, Stratford-upon-Avon, Warwickshire CV37 8BS
Tel: 0789 450123 · Fax: 0789 450472

A magnificent Gothic Mansion situated in 40 acres of glorious grounds. Interiors are striking, note the ceiling in the Drawing Room, the superb fireplace in the entrance Hall, the unique Dining Room with its beautiful panelling and shields. Lovely bedrooms have excellent bathrooms. The exceptional Leisure Complex includes Swimming Pool, Spa Bath, Sauna and Solarium. Matchless facilities are provided for the businessman. Grand, but not stuffy, Ettington Park is a memorable experience.

OPEN: **All year**
NO. ROOMS: **48** EN SUITE **48**
ROOM TELEPHONES: **Yes** TV IN ROOMS: **Yes**
PETS: **No** CHILDREN: **Yes**
DISABLED: **Yes**
LOCATION: **Five miles south of Stratford on A3400**

SWIMMING POOL: **Indoor Heated**
CONFERENCE FACILITIES:
Theatre Style up to 85 Delegates
PRICE GUIDE: SINGLE: **£110**
DOUBLE: **£140** SUITES: **£185**

Stonehouse Court

Bristol Road, Stonehouse, Gloucestershire GL10 3RA
Tel: 0453 825155 · Fax: 0453 824611

Six acres of manicured grounds and gardens surround this mellow Grade 2 listed 17th century Cotswold house. Oak panelling, beams, a massive open fire with dramatic overmantle and comfortable chairs and sofas greet you on arrival in the entrance lounge. More open fires in Cocktail Bar and Restaurant convey an air of warmth and welcome. Lovely bedrooms, some with 4-posters, are beautifully furnished. With its Heli-Pad and matchless facilities for businessmen, Stonehouse Court is a tranquil retreat yet is only one mile from the M5 Motorway.

OPEN: **All year**
NO. ROOMS: **37** EN SUITE **37**
ROOM TELEPHONES: **Yes** TV IN ROOMS: **Yes**
PETS: **No** CHILDREN: **Yes**
DISABLED: **Unsuitable**
LOCATION: **One and a half miles from Jcn 13 on M5**

SWIMMING POOL/HEALTH CLUB: **No**
CONFERENCE FACILITIES:
Exceptional up to 150
PRICE GUIDE:
SINGLE: **£72.50** DOUBLE: **£98**

The Knoll House

Studland Bay, Dorset BH19 3AH
Tel: 092944 251 · Fax: 092944 423

A family hotel par excellence, this fine country house hotel lies in its own attractive grounds which lead to the sea and three miles of golden beaches. Owned and operated by the Ferguson family, Knoll House has every possible amenity to ensure a successful holiday with indoor and outdoor pools, plunge pool, Jacuzzi, steam room, gymnasium and two hard tennis courts. There are six comfortable lounges and a spacious restaurant serving good food and wines. With its adventure playground complete with pirate ship, Knoll House is a self-contained world of its own, where even if it rains, your holiday will still go with a swing.

OPEN: **Easter-October (inc)**
NO. ROOMS: **70** EN SUITE **55**
ROOM TELEPHONES: **Yes** TV IN ROOMS: **Available**
PETS: **Yes** CHILDREN: **Yes**
DISABLED: **Yes**

SWIMMING POOL/HEALTH CLUB: **Yes**
CONFERENCE FACILITIES: **No**

PRICE GUIDE: SINGLE: **£64/£77**
DOUBLE: **£128/£154 (incl Dinner)**

Strattons

Ash Close, Swaffham, Norfolk PE37 7NH
Tel: 0760 23845 · Fax: 0760 23845

This Palladian extravaganza is an intriguing blend of relaxed informality and creative artistry on the part of owners Les & Vanessa Scott. I'm sure if a previous resident, Lady Hamilton, returned today she would approve the ambience. Imagination has been given free reign in the dramatic and stylish decor of the bedrooms. Books, magazines, dried flowers and chinese cats abound in public rooms. Breakfasts are outstanding with freshly squeezed orange, free range eggs, home baked breads and marmalade. Dinner is traditional English and French utilising locally grown produce and herbs from the garden.

OPEN: **All year**
NO. ROOMS: **7** EN SUITE **7**
ROOM TELEPHONES: **Yes** TV IN ROOMS: **Yes**
PETS: **Yes** CHILDREN: **Yes**
DISABLED: **Unsuitable**

SWIMMING POOL/HEALTH CLUB: **No**
CONFERENCE FACILITIES:
Small Business Meetings up to 12
PRICE GUIDE:
SINGLE: **£52** DOUBLE: **£69**

Talland Bay Hotel

Talland-by-Looe, Cornwall PL13 2JB
Tel: 0503 72667 · Fax: 0503 72940

*In these days when so much of the country has been spoiled
by over commercialisation, it is refreshing to arrive at this
old Cornish house in its unspoilt location. The ambience
is one of elegance with well proportioned public rooms
and comfortable furnishings. Bedrooms are individual,
some with 4-posters, sitting rooms, sun terraces and sea
views. In the oak panelled candle-lit Dining
Room you have a choice of table d'hote or a la carte
menus, local specialities include Cornish crab, lobsters
and oysters. Surrounded by sub-tropical plants and
shrubs is a most attractive Swimming Pool. Resident
owners: Major and Mrs Ian Mayman.*

OPEN: **February to December**
NO. ROOMS: **24** EN SUITE **24**
ROOM TELEPHONES: **Yes** TV IN ROOMS: **Yes**
PETS: **Yes** CHILDREN: **Over 5**
DISABLED: **Yes**
LOCATION: **Turn off A387 Looe – Polperro road**

SWIMMING POOL: **Outdoor Heated**
CONFERENCE FACILITIES:
Small Business Meetings up to 30
PRICE GUIDE: SINGLE: **£39.50/£67.50**
DOUBLE: **£80/£154**

Little Silver Country Hotel

Ashford Road, St Michaels, Tenterden, Kent TN30 6SP
Tel: 0233 850321 · Fax: 0233 850647

Every bit as charming as its name, Little Silver is the creation of two dedicated ladies, Rosemary Frith and Dorothy Lawson. This picturesque house nestles in immaculate gardens complete with waterfall. Inside there is an oak beamed 40 foot sitting room with chintzy chairs, an attractive conservatory overlooking the manicured lawns where breakfast is taken and cosy bedrooms with every modern facility. But perhaps its most unusual feature is the unique octagonal conference centre constructed from English oak trees, a favourite venue for many major companies.

OPEN: ***All year***
NO. ROOMS: ***10*** EN SUITE ***10***
ROOM TELEPHONES: ***Yes*** TV IN ROOMS: ***Yes***
PETS: ***By arrangement*** CHILDREN: ***Yes***
DISABLED: ***Yes***
LOCATION: ***Off A28***

SWIMMING POOL/HEALTH CLUB: ***No***
CONFERENCE FACILITIES:
Theatre Style up to 200
PRICE GUIDE:
SINGLE: ***£55/£70*** DOUBLE: ***£70/£100***

Thornbury Castle

Thornbury, Avon BS12 1HH
Tel: 0454 281182 · Fax: 0454 416188

Steeped in history, this magnificent castle dates back to 1511 whose previous residents include Henry VIII, Anne Boleyn and Mary Tudor. Stunning bedchambers are highly individual and feature 4-posters, several huge Tudor fireplaces and oriel windows overlooking the tranquil walled garden. Fine crest emblazoned panelling, antiques and original oil paintings all add to the medieval ambience. Two baronial dining rooms present cuisine of the highest standard and which has earned many accolades for Thornbury Castle. Surrounded by a vineyard, gardens and high walls this is perhaps the ultimate in luxurious period atmosphere.

OPEN: **All year**
NO. ROOMS: **18** EN SUITE **18**
ROOM TELEPHONES: **Yes** TV IN ROOMS: **Yes**
PETS: **No** CHILDREN: **Over 12**

SWIMMING POOL/HEALTH CLUB: **No**
CONFERENCE FACILITIES:
Business Meetings up to 30
PRICE GUIDE:
SINGLE: **£75/£80** DOUBLE: **£95/£195**

Thurlestone Hotel

Thurlestone, Nr Kingsbridge, S Devon TQ7 3NN
Tel: 0548 560382 · Fax: 0548 561069

This imposing hotel overlooking the golf course and the sea, is owned and operated by the Grose family. The entire hotel is furnished and equipped to very high standards, particularly is this so in the bedrooms which have every facility, even to some having videos and private bars. The Restaurant is most attractive with its luxurious drapes and tasteful colour co-ordinated fabrics and looks out to sea. Unrivalled leisure facilities include: Pool Complex, Beauty Salon, Squash, Tennis, Badminton, Golf and Snooker. Staff, many of whom have been with the hotel for years, are courteous and efficient.

OPEN: ***All year***
NO. ROOMS: **68** EN SUITE **68**
ROOM TELEPHONES: ***Yes*** TV IN ROOMS: ***Yes***
PETS: ***Yes*** CHILDREN: ***Yes***
DISABLED: ***Yes***
LOCATION: ***Look for Thurlestone signs off A379***

SWIMMING POOL/HEALTH CLUB:
Indoor/Outdoor & Country Club
CONFERENCE FACILITIES:
Up to 100 theatre style
PRICE GUIDE: SINGLE: ***£60***
      DOUBLE: ***£106/£128***

The Grand Hotel

Seafront, Torquay, Devon TQ2 6NT
Tel: 0803 296677 · Fax: 0803 213462

It is rare to find a hotel of this size that has such an intimate "country house" atmosphere. Perhaps this is because it is privately owned. Bedrooms and suites are a delight and extremely comfortable as are the public areas. In the elegant surroundings of the Restaurant, food of considerable originality from Chef Mel Rumbles and his talented brigade is enhancing the reputation of the Grand. In the Edwardian atmosphere of the Boaters Bar a superb lunchtime buffet is served. With its magnificent leisure facilities and unrivalled marine location, the Grand reigns supreme on the English Riviera.

OPEN: **All year**
NO. ROOMS: **112** EN SUITE **112**
ROOM TELEPHONES: **Yes** TV IN ROOMS: **Yes**
PETS: **Yes** CHILDREN: **Yes**
DISABLED: **By arrangement**
LOCATION: **Follow A380 & signs for Sea Front then turn right**

SWIMMING POOL/HEALTH CLUB:
Indoor/Outdoor
CONFERENCE FACILITIES: **300 theatre style**
PRICE GUIDE:
SINGLE: **£50/£62** DOUBLE: **£80/£120**

The Palace Hotel

Torquay, Devon TQ1 3TG
Tel: 0803 200200 · Fax: 0803 299899

One of the premier hotels of the South West, this former residence of the Bishop of Exeter, is situated in 25 acres of delightful gardens and woodland and has recently been the subject of a major re-furbishment programme. The restaurant serves English and French cuisine, there are 3 bars, and numerous lounges. Notable sporting facilities include, 2 swimming pools, 6 tennis courts (2 indoor), 2 squash courts, golf course and many others. With every facility for Conferences The Palace has something for everyone whether on holiday or business.

OPEN: *All year*
NO. ROOMS: *140* EN SUITE *140*
ROOM TELEPHONES: *Yes* TV IN ROOMS: *Yes*
PETS: *No*   CHILDREN: *Yes*
DISABLED: *Yes*

SWIMMING POOL/HEALTH CLUB: *Yes*
CONFERENCE FACILITIES:
Business meetings up to 260
PRICE GUIDE:
SINGLE: *£70* DOUBLE: *£140*

Alverton Manor

Tregolls Road, Truro, Cornwall TR1 1XQ
Tel: 0872 76633 · Fax: 0872 222989

One of Cornwall's most luxurious hotels, this Grade II listed building is of considerable historical interest. The sun slants through mullioned windows into bedrooms of great charm and individuality. Quiet elegance is the keynote of public rooms with their delightful furnishings and character features combined with designer decor. In the superb dining room you can savour cuisine in the modern English style in the atmosphere of a bygone era. At last, Truro has a hotel of which it can be justly proud.

OPEN: **All year**
NO. ROOMS: **25** EN SUITE **25**
ROOM TELEPHONES: **Yes** TV IN ROOMS: **Yes**
PETS: **No** CHILDREN: **Yes**
DISABLED: **Yes**
LOCATION: **On entering Truro, Hotel is on right of A39**

SWIMMING POOL/HEALTH CLUB: **No**
CONFERENCE FACILITIES: **Business Meetings up to 200 Theatre Style**
PRICE GUIDE:
SINGLE: **£60/£80** DOUBLE: **£80/£100**

Alexander House

Turners Hill, West Sussex RH10 4QD
Tel: 0342 714914 · Fax: 0342 717328

It would be difficult to overdo the superlatives when trying to describe this consumate Mansion set in its own 135 acres of beautifully manicured parkland. The very antithesis of a normal commercial establishment, decor and furnishings are quite dazzling with fabulous antiques, rare textiles and many important paintings. Suites and bedrooms are the very epitome of luxury. In the exquisite elegance of the Dining Room classical cuisine and rare wines can be enjoyed. Live piano music, log fires, breakfast in bed, a chauffeured limousine, all can be savoured in glamourous surroundings for unparalleled splendour.

OPEN: ***All year***
NO. ROOMS: ***14*** EN SUITE ***14***
ROOM TELEPHONES: ***Yes*** TV IN ROOMS: ***Yes***
PETS: ***No*** CHILDREN: ***Over 7***
DISABLED: ***Unsuitable***
LOCATION: ***Off B2110 six miles from Jcn 10 on M23***

SWIMMING POOL/HEALTH CLUB: ***No***
CONFERENCE FACILITIES:
Small Business Meetings up to 12
PRICE GUIDE:
SINGLE: ***£95*** DOUBLE: ***£185/£250***

Ye Olde Dog & Partridge Hotel

High Street, Tutbury, Burton Upon Trent
Tel: 0283 813030 · Fax: 0283 813178

This old 15th century coaching Inn has been the subject of sympathetic restoration over recent years. From its half-timbered facade to its beamed interiors, the Inn oozes character and charm. Immediately adjacent housed in a Georgian building are the bedrooms, reached by an elegant spiral staircase which curves upwards towards a domed roof. Each bedroom is individual in design and furnishing and has every modern facility. Excellent food is served from the carvery, where a pianist plays for dinner. Companies will appreciate the intimate atmosphere of the John of Gaunt meeting room.

OPEN: **All year**
NO. ROOMS: **17** EN SUITE **17**
ROOM TELEPHONES: **Yes** TV IN ROOMS: **Yes**
PETS: **By arrangement** CHILDREN: **Yes**
DISABLED: **Unsuitable**

SWIMMING POOL/HEALTH CLUB: **No**
CONFERENCE FACILITIES:
Up to 12 Boardroom Style
PRICE GUIDE: SINGLE: **£49.50/£59.50**
DOUBLE: **£59.50/£75**

Lords of the Manor

Upper Slaughter, Nr Bourton-on-the-Water, Cheltenham,
Gloucestershire GL54 2JD
Tel: 0451 20243 · Fax: 0451 20696

This grandly named hotel, some parts of which date back to 1650, perhaps most closely approximates to most peoples idea of what a perfect Cotswold Manor should be. Family portraits, log fires and chintzy chairs grace public rooms. In the elegant dining room delicious food and an outstanding wine list combine in an atmosphere of gleaming polished tables and candle light. Bedrooms are supremely comfortable with their pastel shades and fine fabrics, bathrooms are superb. With its parkland setting and private lake, Lords of the Manor is as interesting as its name suggests.

OPEN: **All year**
NO. ROOMS: **29** EN SUITE **29**
ROOM TELEPHONES: **Yes** TV IN ROOMS: **Yes**
PETS: **No** CHILDREN: **Yes**
DISABLED: **Unsuitable**
LOCATION: **Off A429 Stow-Cirencester Road**

SWIMMING POOL/HEALTH CLUB: **No**
CONFERENCE FACILITIES:
Small Business Meetings up to 29
PRICE GUIDE:
SINGLE: **£75** DOUBLE: **From £90**

Woodhayes Country House Hotel

Whimple, Nr Exeter, Devon EX5 2TD
Tel: 0404 822237

Apple orchards and grazing sheep surround this captivating small Georgian Hotel. All public rooms are particularly pleasing with their fresh sunny decor and deep armchairs. Log fires burn in winter, in summer the Sun floods in lighting the elegant interiors. In the pretty Dining Room you will experience excellent country house cooking and enjoy a good night's rest in one of the individually furnished cosy bedrooms. Woodhayes is under the personal supervision of the Rendle family and is ideally located for Exeter.

OPEN: ***All year***
NO. ROOMS: **8** EN SUITE **8**
ROOM TELEPHONES: ***Yes*** TV IN ROOMS: ***Yes***
PETS: ***No*** CHILDREN: ***Over 12***
DISABLED: ***Unsuitable***

SWIMMING POOL/HEALTH CLUB: ***No***
CONFERENCE FACILITIES: ***No***
PRICE GUIDE:
SINGLE: **£75** DOUBLE: **£110 (incl Dinner)**

LOCATION: ***Off A30 signposted Whimple and eight miles from Exeter***

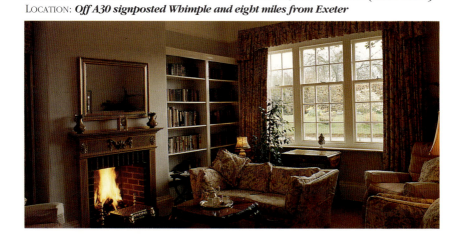

Whitwell Hall
(THIS HOTEL IS NOW NOT OPERATING)

Standing in an elevated position commanding magnificent views of the Vale of York, this imposing Tudor Gothic style mansion is surrounded by its own glorious grounds. Public rooms are well proportioned from the entrance hall with its massive stone pillars, the Drawing Room with log fire and comfortable chairs and settees, to the elegant Dining Room in which you can enjoy excellent food and fine wines. There is a superb Swimming Pool linked to an imaginative Orangery Restaurant and Bar where breakfast and lunch are taken. Resident owners: Mr and Mrs Peter Milner.

OPEN: **All year**
NO. ROOMS: **23** EN SUITE **23**
ROOM TELEPHONES: **Yes** TV IN ROOMS: **Yes**
PETS: **By Arrangement** CHILDREN: **Over 16**
DISABLED: **Yes**
LOCATION: **Off A64 York –Scarborough road, 12 miles from York**

SWIMMING POOL: **Indoor Heated**
CONFERENCE FACILITIES:
Small Business Meetings up to 20
PRICE GUIDE:
SINGLE: **£53/£95** DOUBLE: **£78/£106**

Beechleas

17 Poole Road, Wimborne Minster, Dorset BH21 1QA
Tel: 0202 841684

One cannot fail but be impressed by the standards set at this charming and immaculately maintained small Grade II Georgian town house. Exquisitely furnished bedrooms are thoughtfully appointed with excellent bathrooms, the beamed rooms in the Coach House reflecting a bygone age. Emphasis is on home grown and naturally reared produce cooked by Aga and presented in winter in a delightful dining room with open fire, in summer in a stylish conservatory. Beechleas, in the heart of Thomas Hardy country is owned and operated by Josephine McQuillan.

OPEN: **Closed January**
NO. ROOMS: **7** EN SUITE **7**
ROOM TELEPHONES: **Yes** TV IN ROOMS: **Yes**
PETS: **By arrangement** CHILDREN: **Yes**
DISABLED: **Yes**

SWIMMING POOL/HEALTH CLUB: **No**
CONFERENCE FACILITIES:
Small Business Meetings up to 10
PRICE GUIDE:
SINGLE: **£53/£73** DOUBLE: **£71/£91**

Holbeck Ghyll Country House Hotel

Holbeck Lane, Windermere, Cumbria LA23 1LU
Tel: 05394 32375 · Fax: 05394 34743

The personal attention and friendliness of owners David and Patricia Nicholson contributes in no small measure to the success of this fine country house hotel. Superbly situated in its own delightful grounds looking across Lake Windermere, the house has an interesting history and was once the home of Lord Lonsdale of boxing fame. Pleasing lounges have open fires, books and magazines. Bedrooms, many overlooking the lake, are comfortable with good beds. Food is excellent and is presented with flair in an oak panelled restaurant.

OPEN: **All year**
NO. ROOMS: **14** EN SUITE **14**
ROOM TELEPHONES: **Yes** TV IN ROOMS: **Yes**
PETS: **Yes** CHILDREN: **Yes**
DISABLED: **Unsuitable**
LOCATION: **Off A591 Windermere - Ambleside Rd & turn right signed Troutbeck**

SWIMMING POOL/HEALTH CLUB: **Nearby**
CONFERENCE FACILITIES:
Small Business Meetings up to 14
PRICE GUIDE: SINGLE: **£75**
DOUBLE: **£100/£180 (inc Dinner)**

Cedar Manor

Ambleside Road, Windermere, Cumbria LA23 1AX
Tel: 09662 3192

This charming little Manor, owned and run by the very welcoming Mr and Mrs Hadley, represents excellent value for money. Its unusual lounge has Gothic style arched windows, a unique fireplace and lovely views of the Langdale Pikes. Good home cooking is served in the pleasant Dining Room, whilst in the cosy bedrooms, each individual in design and decor, nothing has been forgotten to ensure guests comfort. Cedar Manor, at the heart of England's Lakeland makes an ideal base for a holiday and won't cost you an "arm and a leg".

OPEN: **All year**
NO. ROOMS: **12** EN SUITE **12**
ROOM TELEPHONES: **Yes** TV IN ROOMS: **Yes**
PETS: **Yes** CHILDREN: **Yes**
DISABLED: **Unsuitable**

SWIMMING POOL/HEALTH CLUB: **No**
CONFERENCE FACILITIES: **No**
PRICE GUIDE:
SINGLE: **£46 (incl Dinner)**
DOUBLE:**£74/£96 (incl Dinner)**

LOCATION: **Quarter mile north of Windermere village on A591 Ambleside Road**

The Old Vicarage

Witherslack, Nr Grange-over-Sands, Cumbria LA11 6RS
Tel: 044852 381 · Fax: 044852 373

In a setting reminiscent of Cezannes painting of Renoirs Garden, we have in this erstwhile Georgian Vicarage a small gem of a hotel. Sometimes the phrase "warm welcome" can be a meaningless cliché but in the case of the Burrington-Brown and Reeve families it is an understatement. Food is simply outstanding, not merely in its imaginative presentation but in the lengths to which the owners go to acquire the finest additive free produce ... note the cheese board! Breakfast was the best I have had anywhere, superlative bacon, free-range eggs, home made everything. Bedrooms vary from comfortable to super luxury. I wish I had more space to do it justice ... just go!

OPEN: **All year**
NO. ROOMS: **14** EN SUITE **14**
ROOM TELEPHONES: **Yes** TV IN ROOMS: **Yes**
PETS: **Yes** CHILDREN: **Yes**
DISABLED: **Yes**

SWIMMING POOL/HEALTH CLUB: **No**
CONFERENCE FACILITIES: **No**
PRICE GUIDE:
  SINGLE: **£58/£78**
  DOUBLE: **£78/£138**

LOCATION: **10 minutes from M6 Jcn 36 just off A590 Kendal-Barrow road**

Halewell Close

Withington, Nr Cheltenham, Gloucestershire GL54 4BN
Tel: 0242 89 238

And now, as they say, for something completely different! This 15th century mellow Cotswold house is the home of Mrs Elizabeth Carey-Wilson, it is not a hotel. Guests dine at one large table and are joined by the hosts. Food is home cooking, roasts and grills. There is a magnificent Drawing Room with huge timbered vaulted ceiling and comfortable bedrooms, one equipped to R.A.D.A.R specifications for disabled guests. Halewell is sited in 50 acres of grounds including a lake, terraces, natural springs and bound by the River Coln.

OPEN: ***All year***
NO. ROOMS: **6** EN SUITE **6**
ROOM TELEPHONES: ***No*** TV IN ROOMS: **Yes**
PETS & CHILDREN: ***By arrangement***
DISABLED: **Yes**

SWIMMING POOL: ***Outdoor Heated***
CONFERENCE FACILITIES: **No**
PRICE GUIDE:
SINGLE: ***£47.50/£51*** DOUBLE: ***£75/£80***

LOCATION: ***Turn off A40 onto A436 at Andoversford going south & 1st left to Withington***

Seckford Hall

Woodbridge, Suffolk, IP13 6NU
Tel: 0394 385678 · Fax: 0394 380610

If one were asked by a visitor from outer space to summon up just one example that best exemplified quintessential England, this historic Tudor Hall would fit the bill. Stunningly picturesque with tall chimneys, fountain, lake and willows. Inside, beams, oak panelling, open fires and period pieces. Bedrooms are full of character, some having 4-posters. There is a superb Lakeside Banqueting Suite with Minstrels Gallery and the fabulous Courtyard Suites are the last word in luxury. The magnificent Tudor Tithe Barn houses a superb air-conditioned Pool with Spa Bath, Gym and Buttery. Owned and run by Michael Bunn.

OPEN: **All year**
NO. ROOMS: **35** EN SUITE **35**
ROOM TELEPHONES: **Yes** TV IN ROOMS: **Yes**
PETS: **Yes** CHILDREN: **Yes**
DISABLED: **By arrangement**
LOCATION: **A12 Woodbridge By-pass direction "Lowestoft"**

SWIMMING POOL/HEALTH CLUB: **Yes**
CONFERENCE FACILITIES:
Theatre Style up to 100, Dining 90
PRICE GUIDE:
SINGLE: **£75/£95** DOUBLE: **£85/£125**

The Feathers Hotel

Market Street, Woodstock, Oxfordshire OX7 1SX
Tel: 0993 812291 · Fax: 0993 813158

This delightful 17th century country house hotel is situated in one of England's most historic towns, notable for Blenheim Palace, birthplace of Sir Winston Churchill. The Feathers exhudes charm with its captivating public rooms, panelled walls, log fires and antiques. Delectable bedrooms are imaginatively designed and furnished, bathrooms are in keeping. The Restaurant is particularly attractive and is noted for its superb cuisine. Staff are welcoming and attentive.

OPEN: **All year**
NO. ROOMS: **17** EN SUITE **16**
ROOM TELEPHONES: **Yes** TV IN ROOMS: **Yes**
PETS: **Yes** CHILDREN: **Yes**
DISABLED: **Unsuitable**

SWIMMING POOL/HEALTH CLUB: **No**
CONFERENCE FACILITIES:
Small Business Meetings up to 20
PRICE GUIDE: SINGLE: **£75/£95**
DOUBLE: **£90/£125** SUITES: **£165**

Watersmeet Hotel

Mortehoe, Woolacombe, North Devon EX34 7EB
Tel: 0271 870333 · Fax: 0271 870890

This country house hotel sits in an elevated position commanding spectacular views of coast and country. In the dramatic setting of the candle-lit Dining Room with its fabulous marine panorama, you can enjoy International cuisine the emphasis being on fresh produce and local speciality dishes. Bedrooms have fresh sunny decor and are most comfortable with every modern facility. Privately owned by Brian and Pat Wheeldon, Watersmeet is one of Devon's finest coastal hotels.

OPEN: *February to December 2nd*
NO. ROOMS: *25* EN SUITE *25*
ROOM TELEPHONES: *Yes* TV IN ROOMS: *Yes*
PETS: *By arrangement* CHILDREN: *Yes*
DISABLED: *Yes*

SWIMMING POOL: *Outdoor Heated*
CONFERENCE FACILITIES:
Business Meetings up to 60
PRICE GUIDE: SINGLE: *£79 (incl Dinner)*
DOUBLE: *£147 (incl Dinner)*

The Old Vicarage Hotel

Worfield, Nr Bridgnorth, Shropshire WV15 5JZ
Tel: 07464 497 · Fax: 07464 552

Owners Peter & Christine Iles have constantly upgraded their former Edwardian parsonage. Situated in a tranquil rural location that may well have inspired Shropshire's famous poet A.E. Houseman into verse, the ambience is relaxed and undemanding. Bedrooms are very well appointed with quality furnishings, those in the Coach House being particularly luxurious and having whirlpool baths. In the elegant Dining Room daily changing menus are based on fresh local produce. The wine list is exceptional.

OPEN: **All year**
NO. ROOMS: **14** EN SUITE **14**
ROOM TELEPHONES: **Yes** TV IN ROOMS: **Yes**
PETS: **Yes** CHILDREN: **Yes**
DISABLED: **Yes**
LOCATION: **Off A454 Bridgnorth – Wolverhampton road**

SWIMMING POOL/HEALTH CLUB: **No**
CONFERENCE FACILITIES:
Small Business Meetings up to 14
PRICE GUIDE:
SINGLE: **£63.50** DOUBLE: **£85/£100**

The Mount Royale

The Mount, York YO2 2DA
Tel: 0904 628856 · Fax: 0904 611171

This has to be one of the most unusual and attractive hotels to be found in a city. Perhaps adjective like intimate and elegant best describe it. The Dining Room is quite enchanting overlooking as it does, lovely old English gardens. A unique feature is a stunning indoor garden with a vast array of exotic plants. Bedrooms are very individual with some fine antique beds. Owned and operated by Richard and Christine Oxtoby, who have, with the Mount Royale, created a beautiful oasis in a historic city.

OPEN: **All year**
NO. ROOMS: **23** EN SUITE **23**
ROOM TELEPHONES: **Yes** TV IN ROOMS: **Yes**
PETS: **By Arrangement** CHILDREN: **Yes**
DISABLED: **Unsuitable**
LOCATION: **On right past Racecourse**

SWIMMING POOL: **Outdoor Heated & Gym**
CONFERENCE FACILITIES:
Small Business Meetings up to 15
PRICE GUIDE: SINGLE: **£62.50/£80**
DOUBLE: **£72.50/£100**
OPEN PLAN SUITES: **£100/£120**

Aldwark Manor Hotel

Aldwark, Alne, York YO6 2NF
Tel: 03473 8146 · Fax: 03473 8867

This impressive 19th century Manor stands in its own 180 acres of peaceful parkland complete with its own golf course. Splendid architectural features abound, note the galleried tromp l'oeil Italianate courtyard and fine fireplace in the hall. With its beautiful furnishings, lovely individually designed bedrooms, many with 4-posters, a delightful restaurant in which to enjoy good food and fine wines and excellent facilities for conferences. Aldwark Manor combines luxury living in an atmosphere of period charm and elegance.

OPEN: **All year**
NO. ROOMS: **20** EN SUITE **20**
ROOM TELEPHONES: **Yes** TV IN ROOMS: **Yes**
PETS: **Yes** CHILDREN: **Yes**
DISABLED: **Yes**

SWIMMING POOL/HEALTH CLUB: **No**
CONFERENCE FACILITIES:
Up to 100 Theatre Style
PRICE GUIDE:
SINGLE: **From £45** DOUBLE: **From £65**

Introduction to the Channel Isles

Hotel L'Horizon

St Brelades Bay, Jersey, Channel Islands
Tel: 0534 43101 · Fax: 0534 46269

This elegant white hotel lies at the apex of St Brelades Beach, a perfect curve of flawless sand washed by clear seas that come right up to the hotel. Bedrooms are luxurious, most with balconies overlooking the water. Immaculate waiters glide beneath crystal chandeliers in the Restaurant. A piano tinkles in the Main Lounge. With its beautiful furnishings and quality fabrics, courteous and highly professional staff, and traditional standards of service and care, little wonder guests return again and again to Hotel L'Horizon.

OPEN: **All year**
NO. ROOMS: **104** EN SUITE **104**
ROOM TELEPHONES: **Yes** TV IN ROOMS: **Yes**
PETS: **No** CHILDREN: **Yes**
DISABLED: **Yes**

SWIMMING POOL/HEALTH CLUB: **Yes**
CONFERENCE FACILITIES:
Business meetings up to 180
PRICE GUIDE:
SINGLE: **£75** DOUBLE: **£150**

The Atlantic Hotel

La Moye, St Brelade, Jersey JE3 8HE
Tel: 0534 44101 · Fax: 0534 44102

Set in its own idyllic gardens with magnificent sea views, for those seeking total peace and quiet this luxurious hotel offers tranquillity in abundance. Elegant bedrooms combine great comfort with every facility. Fabrics and furnishings being tastefully colour co-ordinated throughout. In the delightful restaurant food of exceptional standard is presented by courteous professional staff. There is a superb Palm Club health and leisure centre which includes ozone treated pool, spa pool, mini-gym, fitness studio, sauna and solaria. With its own tennis courts and the championship La Moye Golf Club nearby, you have in the Atlantic a recipe for the perfect holiday.

OPEN: **March-October**
NO. ROOMS: **50** EN SUITE **50**
ROOM TELEPHONES: **Yes** TV IN ROOMS: **Yes**
PETS: **No** CHILDREN: **Yes**
DISABLED: **Yes**

SWIMMING POOL/HEALTH CLUB: **Yes**
CONFERENCE FACILITIES:
Business Meetings up to 50
PRICE GUIDE:
SINGLE: **£75/£100** DOUBLE: **£110/£180**

The Little Grove Hotel

Rue de Haut, St. Lawrence, Jersey, Channel Islands
Tel: 0534 25321 · Fax: 0534 25325

This classic 19th century, pink granite Jersey mansion is one of the Island's finest hotels. The saying "small is beautiful" aptly describes this consummately elegant establishment. Creative cuisine presented by award winning chefs is served in the period atmosphere of the Old Masters Restaurant enhanced by crystal chandeliers. Bedrooms and bathrooms are exquisite. Public rooms are graced by the imaginative use of exposed stone walls, open fires, period pieces and deep soft chairs.

OPEN: **All year**
NO. ROOMS: **13** EN SUITE **13**
ROOM TELEPHONES: **Yes** TV IN ROOMS: **Yes**
PETS: **No** CHILDREN: **Over 12**
DISABLED: **Unsuitable**

SWIMMING POOL: **Heated Outdoor**
CONFERENCE FACILITIES:
Small Business Meetings up to 20
PRICE GUIDE: SINGLE: **£85.50/£109**
DOUBLE: **£117/152.50**
1992 Tariff

Longueville Manor

St Saviour, Jersey JE2 7SA
Tel: 0534 25501 · Fax: 0534 31613

Owned and operated by the Lewis family for 40 years, this is the ultimate in unabashed luxury. A 13th century Manor graced by antiques, beautiful fabrics, exquisite oak panelling, open fires and fresh flower displays. Bedrooms are stunning, furnished with great flair and attention to detail and will surely satisfy the most discerning. Outstanding cuisine based largely on the hotel's own produce is served in two atmospheric dining rooms. Standing in its own 15 acres of tranquil grounds including a lake, Longueville Manor is a peaceful oasis in which to escape the pressures of the 20th century.

OPEN: **All year**
NO. ROOMS: **32** EN SUITE **32**
ROOM TELEPHONES: **Yes** TV IN ROOMS: **Yes**
PETS: **Yes** CHILDREN: **Over 7**
DISABLED: **By arrangement**

SWIMMING POOL: **Outdoor Heated**
CONFERENCE FACILITIES:
Small Business Meetings up to 25
PRICE GUIDE:
SINGLE: **£95/£160** DOUBLE: **£121/£200**

Introduction to Wales

Conrah Country House Hotel

Chancery, Nr Aberystwyth, Dyfed SY23 4DF
Tel: 0970 617941 · Fax: 0970 624546

Standing in its own lovely grounds, this fine Country House Hotel has superb views towards the Cader Idris mountain range. Public rooms have soft chintzy chairs, antiques, log fires and fresh flower arrangements. Good wholesome food is based on fresh Welsh produce whilst the comfortable bedrooms, some in a Courtyard wing are well designed and equipped. Resident owners Mr & Mrs John Heading greet you on arrival and whether on holiday or business, I feel certain you will enjoy your stay at Conrah.

OPEN: *All year*
NO. ROOMS: *20* EN SUITE *19*
ROOM TELEPHONES: *Yes* TV IN ROOMS: *Yes*
PETS: *No* CHILDREN: *Over 5*
DISABLED: *Yes*
LOCATION: *Three miles south of Aberystwyth on A487*

SWIMMING POOL/HEALTH CLUB:
Indoor Heated
CONFERENCE FACILITIES:
Up to 60 theatre style
PRICE GUIDE: SINGLE: *£54* DOUBLE: *£75/£95*

Gliffaes Country House Hotel

Crickhowell, Powys NP8 1RH
Tel: 0874 730371 · Fax: 0874 730463

Owned by the Brabner family since 1948. Gliffaes stands in its own 29 acres of glorious grounds including rare shrubs and specimen trees, a riot of colour in Spring and Summer. One of the foremost fishing hotels in Wales, it has two stretches of water on the world famous River Usk. Public rooms are spacious with log fires in winter. The pleasant Conservatory leads on to the terrace with its dramatic view of the Usk 150 feet below whilst in the Dining Room the accent is on good wholesome food with local specialities. The lunch time cold buffet and afternoon teas are delicious.

OPEN: *Mid-March to end December*
NO. ROOMS: *22* EN SUITE *21*
ROOM TELEPHONES: *Yes* TV IN ROOMS: *No*
PETS: *Lodge only* CHILDREN: *Yes*
DISABLED: *Unsuitable*
LOCATION: *One mile off A40 2¹/₂ miles west of Crickhowell*

SWIMMING POOL/HEALTH CLUB: *No*
CONFERENCE FACILITIES:
Small Business Meetings up to 12/15
PRICE GUIDE:
SINGLE: *£31/£58* DOUBLE: *£62/£92*

Penmaenuchaf Hall

Penmaenpool, Dolgellau, Gwynedd LL40 1YB
Tel: 0341 422129 · Fax: 0341 422129

A recent entrant onto the hotel scene in Wales, Penmaenuchaf Hall already ranks as one of the finest hotels in the country. Surrounded by the Cader Idris mountains overlooking the Mawddach Estuary, this is a civilised retreat for the discerning. Exquisite bedrooms are furnished and equipped to high standards with splendid bathrooms. Great flair is apparent in the choice of furnishings which complement the fine oak panelling and stained glass, enhanced by crackling log fires in winter. Food, including breakfasts, is outstanding with artistically presented dishes to tempt the most jaded palate.

OPEN: **All year**
NO. ROOMS: **14** EN SUITE **14**
ROOM TELEPHONES: **Yes** TV IN ROOMS: **Yes**
PETS: **No** CHILDREN: **Yes**
DISABLED: **Unsuitable**
LOCATION: **Off A493 Dolgellau-Tywyn Road**

SWIMMING POOL/HEALTH CLUB: **No**
CONFERENCE FACILITIES:
Business Meetings up to 100
PRICE GUIDE:
SINGLE: **£40/£95** DOUBLE: **£80/£140**

Dolmelynllyn Hall Hotel

Ganllwyd, Dolgellau, Gwynedd LL40 2HP
Tel: 0341 40273 · Fax: 0341 40273

There is a very pleasing air about Dolmelynllyn Hall, apparent as you enter and are greeted by the very welcoming owners Jon Barkwith and his daughter Jo. The setting is magical. You would have to be dull of soul not to be impressed by the magnificence of the stunning scenery on all sides. Inside, the keynote is relaxed informality. Jo cooks and the accent is on traditional British fare based on small daily changing menus. Bedrooms are each different and there is an appealing conservatory bar and elegant lounge. In an age when so many hotels are chromium plated "sleep 'n eat" factories, Dolmelynllyn Hall is a refreshing antidote.

OPEN: **March to November (inc)**
NO. ROOMS: **11** EN SUITE **11**
ROOM TELEPHONES: **Yes** TV IN ROOMS: **Yes**
PETS: **Yes** CHILDREN: **Over 10**
DISABLED: **Unsuitable**
LOCATION: **Off A470 Dolgellau - Llandudno Rd**

SWIMMING POOL/HEALTH CLUB: **No**
CONFERENCE FACILITIES:
No
PRICE GUIDE:
SINGLE: **£40/£50** DOUBLE: **£80/£100**

Fairyhill

Reynoldston, Gower, W. Glamorgan SA3 1BS
Tel: 0792 390139 · Fax: 0792 391358

It's magic at Fairyhill! Situated in 24 acres of tranquil gardens and woodland. Fairyhill is owned and operated by the very friendly Mr & Mrs Frayne. True Welsh hospitality reigns supreme. Food is superb with an outstanding range of desserts. Bedrooms are cosy with every modern facility and there is a magnificent Coach House with a facility for self-catering. At the heart of the unique Gower peninsula. I can thoroughly recommend this delightful hotel.

OPEN: ***February 1st to November 30th***
NO. ROOMS: ***13*** EN SUITE ***13***
ROOM TELEPHONES: ***Yes*** TV IN ROOMS: ***Yes***
PETS: ***Yes*** CHILDREN: ***Yes*** DISABLED: ***Unsuitable***
LOCATION: ***Exit M4 at Jcn 47. Head for Gorseinon, then Gowerton. Turn right at traffic lights in Gowerton onto B4295. Hotel is 12 miles on left***

SWIMMING POOL/HEALTH CLUB: ***No***
CONFERENCE FACILITIES: ***No***
PRICE GUIDE:
SINGLE: ***£69/£79*** DOUBLE: ***£79/£89***

Llansantffraed Court Hotel

Llanvihangel Gobion, Nr Abergavenny, Gwent
Tel: 0873 840678 · Fax: 0873 840674

This impressive 16th century house is situated in its own 19 acres of peaceful parkland. Approached by a sweeping drive, the imposing stately mansion is particularly appealing with its tall chimneys and dormer windows. Superbly restored, the splendid interiors with their beamed ceilings and open fires, are beautifully furnished. In the kitchen, an all French staff produce creative cuisine presented in the intimate elegance of the restaurant. All bedrooms are delightfully furnished with individual decor, many retaining the original tiled fireplaces. This tranquil retreat is ideally placed for the Wye and Ush Valleys and Brecon Beacons.

OPEN: **All year**
NO. ROOMS: **21** EN SUITE **21**
ROOM TELEPHONES: **Yes** TV IN ROOMS: **Yes**
PETS: **By arrangement** CHILDREN: **Yes**
DISABLED: **Yes**

SWIMMING POOL/HEALTH CLUB: **No**
CONFERENCE FACILITIES:
Theatre Style up to 100
PRICE GUIDE:
SINGLE: **£58/£94** DOUBLE: **£88/£130**

Ty Newydd Country Hotel

Penderyn Road, Hirwaun, Mid Glamorgan CF44 9SX
Tel: 0685 813433 · Fax: 0685 813139

History and the 20th century combine well at Ty Newydd, built by the uncle of Sir Harry Llewellyn of Olympic fame. Bedrooms in the original wing are designed and equipped to high standards with antique pieces and carefully chosen fabrics. Those in the new wing are simpler but equally comfortable. Food is quite superb and is served in an interesting restaurant. Conferences of all sizes are catered for and being situated in the Brecon Beacons, Ty Newydd makes an ideal base for whatever reason you may be staying.

OPEN: ***All year***
NO. ROOMS: ***30*** EN SUITE ***30***
ROOM TELEPHONES: ***Yes*** TV IN ROOMS: ***Yes***
PETS: ***No*** CHILDREN: ***Yes***
DISABLED: ***Yes***
LOCATION: ***Off B4059 Brecon-Hirwaun Road***

SWIMMING POOL/HEALTH CLUB: ***No***
CONFERENCE FACILITIES:
Business Meetings from 30 to 150
PRICE GUIDE:
SINGLE: ***£37.50*** DOUBLE: ***£55/£77***

Lake Vyrnwy Hotel

Lake Vyrnwy, Llanwyddn, Powys SY10 0LY
Tel: 069173 692 · Fax: 069173 259

This impressive hotel commands sensational views of Lake Vyrnwy with its Rhine like tower and panorama of the Berwyn mountain range. Traditional standards of hotel-keeping live on here. Public rooms are reminiscent of a more leisured age like the Drawing Room with its open fire, comfy chairs and Bechstein Grand Piano. Traditionally furnished bedrooms have magnificent views of lake or grounds, some having four posters and Jacuzzis. Daily changing menus feature interesting dishes, much of the produce coming from the 22,000 acre Estate. You will enjoy the food that is, if you can wrench your eyes away from the dramatic views. For sportsmen, Lake Vyrnwy is a positive Mecca, and there is an excellent tennis court.

OPEN: **All year**
NO. ROOMS: **30** EN SUITE **30**
ROOM TELEPHONES: **Yes** TV IN ROOMS: **Yes**
PETS: **Yes** CHILDREN: **Yes**
DISABLED: **Unsuitable**
LOCATION: **35 miles due west of Shewsbury in the Berwyn Mountains**

SWIMMING POOL/HEALTH CLUB: **No**
CONFERENCE FACILITIES: **Up to 30**
PRICE GUIDE:
SINGLE: **£55** DOUBLE: **£78/£137.50**

The West Arms Hotel

Llanarmon, Dyffryn Ceiriog, Nr Llangollen, Clwyd LL20 7LD
Tel: 069176 665 · Fax: 069176 622

This 400 year old atmospheric Welsh Inn lies in an unspoilt valley surrounded by gently undulating hills. Blackened beams, stone flagged floors, chintzy chairs, inglenooks and a welcoming log fire blazing in the Hall, you might think you have stepped back in time. Good food, fine wines and cosy bedrooms, this is the West Arms, a pastoral idyll where sheep outnumber people. As an "away from it all" location, yet with easy access from all major routes and motorways, this charming old Inn is hard to beat.

OPEN: **All year**
NO. ROOMS: **14** EN SUITE **14**
ROOM TELEPHONES: **Yes** TV IN ROOMS: **Some**
PETS: **Yes** CHILDREN: **Yes**
DISABLED: **Yes**

SWIMMING POOL/HEALTH CLUB: **No**
CONFERENCE FACILITIES:
Small Business Meetings up to 25
PRICE GUIDE: SINGLE: **£54.50/£59.50**
DOUBLE: **£86/£91**

LOCATION: **Off A5 at Chirk & follow B4500 for 11 miles, then follow Ceirog Valley signs**

St. Tudno Hotel

Promenade, Llandudno, Gwynedd LL30 2LP
Tel: 0492 874411 · Fax: 0492 860407

It is rare to find in a resort, a small hotel as individual and appealing as the St. Tudno. Interiors are very glamorous, from the air-conditioned Garden Room Restaurant, where it feels like Summer all the year round, to the exquisitely appointed bedrooms with their sumptuous drapes, rich fabrics and furnishings. This small gem is owned and operated by Martin and Janette Bland whose dedication to the art of hotel-keeping has earned many accolades for St. Tudno. Staff are courteous and attentive.

OPEN: **All year**
NO. ROOMS: **21** EN SUITE **21**
ROOM TELEPHONES: **Yes** TV IN ROOMS: **Yes**
PETS: **By arrangement** CHILDREN: **Yes**
DISABLED: **By arrangement**
LOCATION: **On Seafront opposite Pier**

SWIMMING POOL: **Indoor Heated**
CONFERENCE FACILITIES:
Small Business Meetings up to 12
PRICE GUIDE:
SINGLE: **£55/£65** DOUBLE: **From £75**

The Lake Country House

Llangammarch Wells, Powys LD4 4BS
Tel: 05912 202 and 474 · Fax: 05912 457

Standing in its own 50 acres of beautiful grounds with towering rhododendrons, impressive specimen trees, riverside walks and a trout-filled lake, this delightful hotel epitomises all that is best in the Country House Hotel. Owned and operated by Mr & Mrs Mifsud, you will be cosseted in artistically designed bedrooms (9 are suites) every one individual. Public rooms are particularly spacious, the impressive Dining Room and Hall having log fires. Cuisine is of exceptionally high standard, dishes are inventive and presented with flair. The wine list is outstanding with over 300 bins.

OPEN: *All year*
NO. ROOMS: *18* EN SUITE *18*
ROOM TELEPHONES: *Yes* TV IN ROOMS: *Yes*
PETS: *Yes* CHILDREN: *Over 8*
DISABLED: *Yes*
LOCATION: *Off A483 six miles from Builth Wells*

SWIMMING POOL/HEALTH CLUB: *No*
CONFERENCE FACILITIES:
Small Business Meetings up to 20
PRICE GUIDE:
SINGLE: *£75* DOUBLE: *£95/£115*

Llangoed Hall

Llyswen, Brecon, Powys LD3 0YP
Tel: 0874 754525 · Fax: 0874 754545

One of Britain's finest Country House Hotels restored and refurbished regardless of cost by Sir Bernard Ashley of Laura Ashley fame, this distinguished Edwardian house successfully manages to re-create a house party atmosphere. Superb bedrooms and suites are furnished with taste and style. In the Great Hall a log fires burns. Public rooms are supremely comfortable with their colour co-ordinated fabrics and furnishings. A unique collection of original paintings look down on fine oriental rugs and antiques whilst in the Dining Room inventive and imaginative classical cuisine is supported by an outstanding wine list of 300 bins. An exquisite oasis of good living in idyllic surroundings.

OPEN: **All year**
NO. ROOMS: **23** EN SUITE **23**
ROOM TELEPHONES: **Yes** TV IN ROOMS: **Yes**
PETS: **In heated kennels** CHILDREN: **Over 8**
DISABLED: **Unsuitable**
LOCATION: **Off A470 eleven miles north of Brecon**

SWIMMING POOL/HEALTH CLUB:
No
CONFERENCE FACILITIES: **Up to 26**
PRICE GUIDE:
SINGLE: **£105/£175** DOUBLE: **£130/£295**

The Celtic Manor Hotel

Coldra Woods, Newport, Gwent NP6 2YA
Tel: 0633 413000 · Fax: 0633 412910

Although dating back centuries and with recent additions, this fine house retains many original features, a magnificent oak staircase and panelling, superb stained glass windows and great fireplaces. Luxurious bedrooms have splendid bathrooms and there are two restaurants serving fine food and wines. Allied to a fabulous swimming pool are a comprehensively equipped gymnasium and matchless facilities for business meetings and conferences. Surrounded by 300 acres of hills and woods, Celtic Manor stands as one of Wales premier hotels.

OPEN: **All year**
NO. ROOMS: **73** EN SUITE **73**
ROOM TELEPHONES: **Yes** TV IN ROOMS: **Yes**
PETS: **No** CHILDREN: **Yes**
DISABLED: **Unsuitable**
LOCATION: **From Jcn 24 on M4 Hotel is 400 yds along A48 signed Newport**

SWIMMING POOL/HEALTH CLUB: **Yes**
CONFERENCE FACILITIES:
Business Meetings from 10-300
PRICE GUIDE:
SINGLE: **£85** DOUBLE: **£99 (Room Only)**

Penally Abbey

Penally, S. Pembrokeshire
Tel: 0834 843033 · Fax: 0834 844714

This charming Gothic style country house lies in an idyllic setting with the glittering sea beyond, its own 5 acres containing a ruined Chapel and Wishing Well. You might consider visiting the Well and wishing that you can find other small gems like Penally. Owners, Mr and Mrs Warren go out of their way to ensure your well being, breakfast can even be taken as late as 11 a.m. How's that for personal service! The delightful bedrooms (some with 4-posters) have many thoughtful extras, bathrooms are excellent. Dinner cooked by Mrs Warren utilising fresh produce is served in a romantic candle-lit Dining Room, amidst the gleam of polished wood and crystal chandeliers.

OPEN: **All year**
NO. ROOMS: **10** EN SUITE **10**
ROOM TELEPHONES: **Yes** TV IN ROOMS: **Yes**
PETS: **No** CHILDREN: **Yes**
DISABLED: **Yes**
LOCATION: **Off the A4139 Tenby – Pembroke coast road**

SWIMMING POOL/HEALTH CLUB: **No**
CONFERENCE FACILITIES:
Small Business Meetings up to 12
PRICE GUIDE: SINGLE: **£80 (incl Dinner)**
DOUBLE: **£118/£132 (incl Dinner)**

The Hotel Portmerion

Portmerion, Gwynedd LL48 6ET
Tel: 0766 770228 · Fax: 0766 771331

An Italianate fantasy village, the dream come true of architect Sir Clough Williams-Ellis. At the heart of the village stands this highly distinctive hotel, restored to its former glory. Stunning without and exotic within, notable past clients include Noel Coward, H.G. Wells, G.B. Shaw and Bertrand Russell. Strikingly stylish in decor with dazzling features, i.e. elaborate furniture from Rajasthan, a hand carved fireplace, huge sparkling gilt mirrors and sumptuous rich drapes. Fabulous bedroom suites are luxurious and flamboyantly individual with superb views of Portmerion and the estuary. Add to this food of great originality and you have in Hotel Portmerion a unique and magical experience.

OPEN: **February to January 5th**
NO. ROOMS: **34** EN SUITE **34**
ROOM TELEPHONES: **Yes** TV IN ROOMS: **Yes**
PETS: **No** CHILDREN: **Yes**
DISABLED: **Unsuitable**
LOCATION: **Off A487 Penrhyndeudraeth – Porthmadog road**

SWIMMING POOL: **Outdoor Heated**
CONFERENCE FACILITIES:
Theatre Style up to 100
PRICE GUIDE:
SINGLE: **£57/£136** DOUBLE: **£67/£146**

St Brides Hotel

Saundersfoot, Dyfed SA69 9NH
Tel: 0834 812304 · Fax: 0834 813303

Standing in an elevated position overlooking Camarthen Bay, St Brides commands superb views, in particular from its air conditioned cliff top Commodore Restaurant. Locally caught fish features prominently on the varied menus. Bedrooms (some with 4-posters) have every modern facility and there are five impressive suites. Afficianades of Dylan Thomas will appreciate Kaptain Katz'z drinks salon with its solid oak bar and leaded light windows. In addition there are three fully equipped conference suites, all air conditioned.

OPEN: **All year**
NO. ROOMS: **45** EN SUITE **45**
ROOM TELEPHONES: **Yes** TV IN ROOMS: **Yes**
PETS: **Yes** CHILDREN: **Yes**
DISABLED: **Yes**
LOCATION: **Take A477 from St Clear or A476 from Fishguard**

SWIMMING POOL: **Outdoor Heated**
CONFERENCE FACILITIES:
Business Meetings from 20 to 120
PRICE GUIDE:
SINGLE: **£56** DOUBLE: **£87** SUITES: **£130**

Warpool Court Hotel

St Davids, Pembrokeshire SA62 6BN
Tel: 0437 720300 · Fax: 0437 720676

Two stone figures gaze out across the sea from the grounds of this beautifully situated hotel, adding to the timeless feeling of tranquillity which permeates this historic region. A feature of Warpool Court is the unique collection of some 3,000 armorial and ornamental tiles scattered throughout the hotel. Situated immediately adjacent to the famous Pembrokeshire Coastal Path, the hotel offers good food based on fresh produce, comfortable bedrooms, and lounges in which open fires burn in winter. An ideal spot for family holidays with courteous attention from friendly staff.

OPEN: **5th February to end December**
NO. ROOMS: **25** EN SUITE **25**
ROOM TELEPHONES: **Yes** TV IN ROOMS: **Yes**
PETS: **Yes** CHILDREN: **Yes**
DISABLED: **Unsuitable**
LOCATION: **Turn off A487 in St Davids Hotel is signed off to left**

SWIMMING POOL: **Covered Outdoor (Easter - Oct)**
CONFERENCE FACILITIES:
Small Business Meetings up to 25
PRICE GUIDE:
SINGLE: **£44/£62** DOUBLE: **£78/£120**

Introduction to Scotland

©Oxford Cartographers

Summer Isles Hotel

Achiltibuie, Ross-shire IV26 2YG
Tel: 085482 282

In a dramatic wilderness of sea and mountains facing a straggle of islands from which the hotel takes its name, you will enjoy unusual standards of civilised creature comforts. Food is outstanding. Everything home produced or caught locally and there is a superb selection of wines and one of the best cheese boards I have ever seen. Run by Mark and Geraldine Irvine, the hotel is relaxed and undemanding and forms an excellent base for nature lovers who must feel that this is "paradise found" if Milton will forgive me!

OPEN: **Easter to Mid-October**
NO. ROOMS: **11** EN SUITE **11**
ROOM TELEPHONES: **No** TV IN ROOMS: **No**
PETS: **Yes** CHILDREN: **Over 8**
DISABLED: **Unsuitable**
LOCATION: **25 miles North of Ullapool**

SWIMMING POOL/HEALTH CLUB: **No**
CONFERENCE FACILITIES: **No**
PRICE GUIDE:
SINGLE: **£44/£60**
DOUBLE: **£63/£87**

Invercreran Country House Hotel

Glen Creran, Appin, Argyll PA38 4BJ
Tel: 063173 414 & 456 · Fax: 063173 532

This is a most unusual and appealing small hotel which commands what has to be one of the most sensational mountain views in Scotland. Public rooms are aesthetically pleasing like the delightful lounge with its free-standing log fire surmounted by a copper canopy, and the dramatic semi-circular dining room with its emphasis on local sea food and Scottish produce backed by an extensive wine list. Luxurious bedrooms complete the picture and you will be welcomed by the very friendly Kersley family.

OPEN: *March 1st to Mid-November*
NO. ROOMS: *9* EN SUITE *9*
ROOM TELEPHONES: *Yes* TV IN ROOMS: *Yes*
PETS: *In Kennels* CHILDREN: *Over 5*
DISABLED: *Unsuitable*
LOCATION: *Half mile off A828 Oban to Fort William road*

SWIMMING POOL/HEALTH CLUB: *No*
CONFERENCE FACILITIES: *No*
PRICE GUIDE:
SINGLE: *£80 (incl Dinner)*
DOUBLE: *£140/£160 (incl Dinner)*

Arisaig House

Beasdale, by Arisaig, Inverness-shire PH39 4NR
Tel: 06875 622 · Fax: 06875 626

As a soothing antidote to the pressures of the modern world one could hardly improve on a sojourn at Arisaig House. It is an oasis of peace surrounded by grounds which contain many varieties of azalea, rhododendron and roses and where great Sequoia and Wellingtonia trees flank the drive. Elegant public rooms with crackling log fires, beautifully furnished and well appointed bedrooms and the finest of food presented in a candle-lit panelled Dining Room, assure your well being. Your hosts, Ruth and John and Andrew Smither.

OPEN: **March to November**
NO. ROOMS: **15** EN SUITE **13 (2 private)**
ROOM TELEPHONES: **Yes** TV IN ROOMS: **Yes**
PETS: **No** CHILDREN: **Over 10**
DISABLED: **Unsuitable**
LOCATION: **On A830 three miles east of Arisaig**

SWIMMING POOL/HEALTH CLUB: **No**
CONFERENCE FACILITIES: **No**
PRICE GUIDE:
SINGLE: **£49.50/£95**
DOUBLE: **£110/£215**

Balcary Bay Hotel

Auchencairn, Nr Castle Douglas, Kirkcudbrightshire DG7 1QZ
Tel: 055664 217

Overlooking the erstwhile smugglers haunt of Heston Isle, with grounds reaching to the waters edge, this pleasing small hotel has superb views of the Solway Coast and Cumbrian Mountains. Owned and operated by the Lamb family, you will find comfortable bedrooms, many with lovely views of the Bay and good Scottish food with local specialities, try the Balcary Bay salmon. This romantic part of Galloway has largely escaped mass tourism and if it was favoured by Robert Burns, Sir Walter Scott and John Buchan, I'm sure you too will like it.

OPEN: **Early March to end November**
NO. ROOMS: **17** EN SUITE **17**
ROOM TELEPHONES: **Yes** TV IN ROOMS: **Yes**
PETS: **Yes** CHILDREN: **Yes**
DISABLED: **Unsuitable**
LOCATION: **Two miles from village off A711**

SWIMMING POOL/HEALTH CLUB:
No
CONFERENCE FACILITIES: **No**
PRICE GUIDE:
SINGLE: **£38/£45** DOUBLE: **£75/£85**

Auchterarder House

Auchterarder, Perthshire PH3 1DZ
Tel: 0764 63646 · Fax: 0764 62939

This is a quite magnificent house with stunning public rooms situated within 17 acres of lovely grounds containing rare shrubs and specimen trees. Note the superb panelling, marble foyer and elegant conservatory. A supreme example of Victorian splendour with many elaborate and ornate features. Food is quite superb as is the warmth of welcome accorded by Audrey and Ian Brown and their sons. A mere two miles from the world famous Gleneagles Golf Courses, this is one of my top recommendations in bonnie Scotland.

OPEN: *All year*
NO. ROOMS: *15* EN SUITE *15*
ROOM TELEPHONES: *Yes* TV IN ROOMS: *Yes*
PETS: *Yes*   CHILDREN: *Over 10*
DISABLED: *Yes*
LOCATION: *Near Gleneagles on B8062*

SWIMMING POOL/HEALTH CLUB: *No*
CONFERENCE FACILITIES:
Small Executive Business Meetings
PRICE GUIDE: SINGLE: *£90/£110*
                    DOUBLE: *£130/£195*

Fairfield House Hotel

Fairfield Road, Ayr KA7 2AR
Tel: 0292 267461 · Fax: 0292 261456

This Mansion House, the former home of a Glasgow Tea Merchant, is now a luxurious hotel. Lady Henrietta Spencer Churchill is responsible for the striking interiors. In the main house bedrooms are particularly spacious with some of the finest bathrooms to be found in the country, those in the annexe being much simpler. Imaginatively presented dishes can be enjoyed in the luxurious surroundings of the restaurant. Businessmen are especially well catered for and everything is backed by concerned personal service and attention to detail.

OPEN: *All year*
NO. ROOMS: *31* EN SUITE *31*
ROOM TELEPHONES: *Yes* TV IN ROOMS: *Yes*
PETS: *Yes* CHILDREN: *Yes*
DISABLED: *Yes*

SWIMMING POOL/HEALTH CLUB: *Yes*
CONFERENCE FACILITIES:
Small Business Meetings up to 50
PRICE GUIDE:
SINGLE: *£70* DOUBLE: *£90*

Auchen Castle

Beattock, by Moffat, Dumfries-shire DG10 9SH
Tel: 0683 407 · Fax: 0683 667

In a magnificent elevated position situated within its own 50 acres of glorious grounds overlooking a panorama of mountain and woodland, this impressive Scottish Baronial Mansion offers excellent value for money. Good home cooking and comfortable accommodation make this a perfect stop over whether going North or South. In this, the land of Robbie Burns and Sir Walter Scott you will be warmly welcomed by resident owners, Mr & Mrs Bob Beckh.

OPEN: **All year**
NO. ROOMS: **25** EN SUITE **25**
ROOM TELEPHONES: **Yes** TV IN ROOMS: **Yes**
PETS: **Yes** CHILDREN: **Yes**
DISABLED: **Unsuitable**
LOCATION: **Access direct from A74 one mile north of Beattock Village**

SWIMMING POOL/HEALTH CLUB: **No**
CONFERENCE FACILITIES:
Small Business Meetings up to 30
PRICE GUIDE:
SINGLE: **£48** DOUBLE: **£54/£68**

Shieldhill Country House Hotel

Quothquan, Biggar, Lanarkshire ML12 6NA
Tel: 0899 20035 · Fax: 0899 21092

Undoubtedly one of the most attractive hotels in the Borders, this lovely Country House Hotel is a monument to good taste. Interiors have been designed with great flair and imagination by the owners Christine Dunstan and Jack Greenwald utilising Laura Ashley prints and fabrics. Superb bedrooms, some with 4 posters, Jacuzzis and fireplaces are individually designed, each with a Scottish battle theme. Warm panelling, log fires, soft chairs and exquisite drapes grace public rooms. Retaining the atmosphere of a bygone era Shieldhill warrants its place amongst Scotland's finest hotels.

OPEN: **March 1st to December 31st**
NO. ROOMS: **11** EN SUITE **11**
ROOM TELEPHONES: **Yes** TV IN ROOMS: **Yes**
PETS: **No** CHILDREN: **Over 12**
DISABLED: **Unsuitable**
LOCATION: **Follow signs for Shieldhill House from Biggar**

SWIMMING POOL/HEALTH CLUB: **No**
CONFERENCE FACILITIES:
Small Business Meetings up to 14
PRICE GUIDE: SINGLE: **£85/£130**
DOUBLE: **From £98/£165**

Borthwick Castle

North Middleton, Midlothian EH23 4QY
Tel: 0875 20514 · Fax: 0875 21702

You really are stepping back in time when you enter Borthwick. No pseudo castle this! Dating from 1430 with 20 foot thick walls, the Castle rises abruptly dominant, a great tower massively impressive. In the Great Hall with its colossal 40 foot Gothic Arch, Minstrel Gallery and mighty hooded fireplace, you will feel you have been transported back in time as you dine by firelight and candlelight. Bedchambers have 20th century appointments but echo the days when occupied by Mary Queen of Scots and Bothwell. Dungeons, battlements, a chapel, combine to form a unique experience. There's nothing quite like it!

OPEN: **All year**
NO. ROOMS: **10** EN SUITE **10**
ROOM TELEPHONES: **Yes** TV IN ROOMS: **Yes**
PETS: **No** CHILDREN: **Yes**
DISABLED: **Unsuitable**
LOCATION: **Signposted off A7 twelve miles South of Edinburgh**

SWIMMING POOL/HEALTH CLUB: **No**
CONFERENCE FACILITIES:
Small Business Meetings up to 60
PRICE GUIDE:
SINGLE: **£75** DOUBLE: **£165**

Nivingston House

Cleish Hills, Nr Kinross, Kinross-shire KY13 7LS
Tel: 05775 216 · Fax: 05775 238

Owned by Allan & Pat Deeson (see also under Perth) this attractive hotel nestles at the foot of the Cleish Hills. Award winning chefs have created an enviable reputation for Nivingston House with delicious daily changing menus. Decor throughout the hotel is truly delightful with tasteful colour co-ordinated fabrics by Laura Ashley in both public rooms and the charming bedrooms. An absolutely ideal location whether you are touring or on business.

OPEN: *All year*
NO. ROOMS: *17* EN SUITE *17*
ROOM TELEPHONES: *Yes* TV IN ROOMS: *Yes*
PETS: *Yes* CHILDREN: *Yes*
DISABLED: *Yes*
LOCATION: *Five miles from M90 Junction 5*

SWIMMING POOL/HEALTH CLUB: *No*
CONFERENCE FACILITIES:
Small Business Meetings up to 15
PRICE GUIDE:
SINGLE: *£75* DOUBLE: *£90/£120*

Contin House

Contin, by Strathpeffer, Ross-shire IV14 9EB
Tel: 0997 421920 · Fax: 0997 421841

Concerned personal service is perhaps only possible in a small privately owned establishment like Contin House. Owners David and Daphne Du Boulay go out of their way to ensure their guests comfort. Superb home cooking using only the finest local ingredients form the basis of thoughtful small menus. Vegetables are from the walled garden whenever possible and you eat in a cosy candle-lit dining room. Log fires, comfortable bedrooms, a peaceful Highland setting and good company, this then is Contin House.

OPEN: *1st March-November 30th*
NO. ROOMS: *5* EN SUITE *5*
ROOM TELEPHONES: *Yes* TV IN ROOMS: *Yes*
PETS: *Yes* CHILDREN: *Over 8*
DISABLED: *Unsuitable*

SWIMMING POOL/HEALTH CLUB: *No*
CONFERENCE FACILITIES:
Small Business Meetings up to 10
PRICE GUIDE: SINGLE: *£47.25/£62.50*
DOUBLE: *£94.50/£125 (inc Dinner)*

LOCATION: *Follow sign for "Contin Burial Ground" at east end of village*

Enmore Hotel

Marine Parade, Kirn, Dunoon, Argyll
Tel: 0369 2230 · Fax: 0369 2148

The intention of hosts Angela and David Wilson is to ensure their guests feel welcome. Directly facing the Bay the hotel has pretty colourful bedrooms, many overlooking the water some with whirlpool baths and have thoughtful extras like fresh flowers, chocolates and towelling robes. "Taste of Scotland" dishes feature on the interesting menus and afterwards relax in one of three elegant lounges. This attractive house makes the perfect base for touring the Western Highlands.

OPEN: **All year**
NO. ROOMS: **11** EN SUITE **11**
ROOM TELEPHONES: **Yes** TV IN ROOMS: **Yes**
PETS: **Yes** CHILDREN: **Yes**
DISABLED: **Unsuitable**
LOCATION: **On the A815 coastal road of Dunoon**

SWIMMING POOL/HEALTH CLUB: **No**
CONFERENCE FACILITIES:
Small Business Meetings up to 16
PRICE GUIDE:
SINGLE: **£40** DOUBLE: **£80/£120**

Channings

South Learmonth Gardens, Edinburgh EH4 1EZ
Tel: 031 315 2226 · Fax: 031 332 9631

This assemblage of five Edwardian Townhouses in a quiet cobbled street just a stroll from the city centre, is just the opposite from the bland impersonality of the average city centre hotel. Cosy, and with a "club" like atmosphere, Channings has a delightful intimate feel with its charming bedrooms, oak panelled library, antiques, objects d'art and the relaxed ambience of comfortable lounges with their open fires. The elegant Brasserie is a popular venue for locals and residents and serves succulent food at reasonable prices. The halcyon calm makes this an ideal venue for company meetings.

OPEN: **All year**
NO. ROOMS: **48** EN SUITE **48**
ROOM TELEPHONES: **Yes** TV IN ROOMS: **Yes**
PETS: **No** CHILDREN: **Yes**
DISABLED: **Unsuitable**

SWIMMING POOL/HEALTH CLUB: **No**
CONFERENCE FACILITIES:
Small Business Meetings up to 20
PRICE GUIDE:
SINGLE: **£69/£98** DOUBLE: **£95/£145**

Castleton House

Eassie, Glamis, by Forfar, Angus DD8 1SJ
Tel: 030784 340 · Fax: 030784 506

The saying "small is beautiful" is particularly appropriate when applied to this small luxury hotel operated by owner Chef William Little. A magnificent galleried hall leads to supremely comfortable bedrooms, furnished with great taste. Cuisine is memorable and has earned a justifiable reputation. A mecca for sportsmen, Castleton House is ideally placed for world famous Golf Courses like St. Andrews, Gleneagles, Rosemount and Carnoustie and for the businessman is a delightful alternative to soul-less "sleep and eat" factories.

OPEN: *All year*
NO. ROOMS: **6** EN SUITE **6**
ROOM TELEPHONES: *Yes* TV IN ROOMS: *Yes*
PETS: *In kennels* CHILDREN: *Yes*
DISABLED: *Unsuitable*
LOCATION: *Off A94 at Glamis*

SWIMMING POOL/HEALTH CLUB: *No*
CONFERENCE FACILITIES: *No*
PRICE GUIDE:
SINGLE: *From £60*
DOUBLE: *From £90*

One Devonshire Gardens

Glasgow G12 0UX
Tel: 041 339 2001 · Fax: 041 337 1663

This unusual and highly personal small hotel has been designed with considerable flair and imagination by owner Ken McCulloch. Bedrooms are luxurious, very individual with excellent bathrooms. Public rooms are quite magnificent with many period features, not least the impressive dining room in which only the finest cuisine is presented on fine bone china in an atmosphere of candle light combined with discreet courteous service. Quietly located in a tree lined terrace, this charming Victorian town house is a mere 10 minutes from the city centre.

OPEN: **All year**
NO. ROOMS: **27** EN SUITE **27**
ROOM TELEPHONES: **Yes** TV IN ROOMS: **Yes**
PETS: **By arrangement** CHILDREN: **Yes**
DISABLED: **Unsuitable**

SWIMMING POOL/HEALTH CLUB: **No**
CONFERENCE FACILITIES:
Small Business Meetings up to 20
PRICE GUIDE:
SINGLE: **£125/£135** DOUBLE: **£145/£155**

LOCATION: **From city centre take Anniesland Rd, left into Hyndland Rd, 1st left into Hughenden Rd**

Glenborrodale Castle

Glenborrodale, Acharacle, Argyll PH36 4JP
Tel: 09724 266 · Fax: 09724 224

Magnificent and impressive are sometimes overworked adjectives, but not when applied to Glenborrodale Castle, restored by millionaire Peter de Savary. One arrives via a single track road feeling much as the travellers must have felt on arriving finally in Shangri-la! Tranquillity and seclusion abound amidst its 1,000 acres of mountain and loch scenery. Public rooms are stunning, bedrooms charming and individual with every modern convenience. All is perhaps best summed up with a quote by Robert Burns from the hotels' brochure. "In heaven itself I'll ask no more than just a Highland welcome".

OPEN: **Easter to October 31st**
NO. ROOMS: **16** EN SUITE **16**
ROOM TELEPHONES: **Yes** TV IN ROOMS: **Yes**
PETS: **In kennels** CHILDREN: **Yes**
DISABLED: **Unsuitable**
LOCATION: **On B8007, 41 miles west of Fort William**

HEALTH CLUB: **Yes**
CONFERENCE FACILITIES:
Small Business Meetings
PRICE GUIDE:
SINGLE: **£100/£120** DOUBLE: **£150/£250**

Culloden House

Culloden, Inverness IV1 2NZ
Tel: 0463 790461 · Fax: 0463 792181

This imposing Georgian Mansion, once the battle headquarters of Bonnie Prince Charlie, is now the home of Ian and Marjory McKenzie who cosset their guests in an atmosphere of period elegance. Ornate Adam style plasterwork enhances the Drawing Room, whilst in the Adam Dining Room superb Scottish food is beautifully presented. Vegetarians are also well catered for. Fine crystal chandeliers grace public rooms and bedrooms have every convenience with en suite showers, whirlpool baths, four-posters and king size beds. The Garden Wing of non-smoking rooms are quite superb.

OPEN: **All year**
NO. ROOMS: **25** EN SUITE **25**
ROOM TELEPHONES: **Yes** TV IN ROOMS: **Yes**
PETS: **By arrangement** CHILDREN: **Over 10**
DISABLED: **Unsuitable**
LOCATION: **Take A96 from Inverness and turn to sign for Culloden**

SWIMMING POOL/HEALTH CLUB: **No**
CONFERENCE FACILITIES:
Small Business Meetings up to 45
PRICE GUIDE: SINGLE: **£110**
DOUBLE: **£150/£190**

Bunchrew House Hotel

Inverness IV3 6TA
Tel: 0463 234917 · Fax: 0463 710620

A particularly friendly and relaxed atmosphere prevail at this fine 17th century Scottish Mansion peacefully located on the shores of the Beauly Firth within its own 15 acres of wooded gardens. Owners Alan and Patsy Wilson extend true Scottish hospitality in an ambience of warm panelling and log fires. Each bedroom is individual in character, with a mixture of 4-posters, half testers and Jacuzzi baths, all are appointed and furnished to the highest standards. In the lovely dining room local Scottish produce forms the basis of succulent dishes.

OPEN: ***All year***
NO. ROOMS: ***11*** EN SUITE ***11***
ROOM TELEPHONES: ***Yes*** TV IN ROOMS: ***Yes***
PETS: ***By arrangement*** CHILDREN: ***Yes***
DISABLED: ***Yes***
LOCATION: ***Off A862 Inverness-Beauly Road***

SWIMMING POOL/HEALTH CLUB: ***No***
CONFERENCE FACILITIES:
Up to 100 Theatre Style
PRICE GUIDE:
SINGLE: ***£55/£82*** DOUBLE: ***£75/£115***

Dunain Park
Inverness IV3 6JN
Tel: 0463 230512 · Fax: 0463 224532

This attractive small hotel situated within its own six acres of delightful grounds is owned and operated by Mr and Mrs Nicoll. Bedrooms are appointed to high standards and suites in the new wing are superb with king size beds and Italian marble tiled bathrooms. Two Cottage Suites 100 yards from the hotel are equipped to the same standards. Public rooms are furnished with antiques, original oil paintings and have log fires. In the intimate atmosphere of the Dining Rooms you will enjoy good food and fine wines.

OPEN: **All year**
NO. ROOMS: **14** EN SUITE **14**
ROOM TELEPHONES: **Yes** TV IN ROOMS: **Yes**
PETS: **Yes** CHILDREN: **Yes**
DISABLED: **Yes**
LOCATION: **Just off A82 Fort William road three miles out of Inverness**

SWIMMING POOL: **Yes**
CONFERENCE FACILITIES:
Small Business Meetings
PRICE GUIDE:
SINGLE: **£80/£100** DOUBLE: **£110/£140**

Ardanaiseig

Kilchrenan, by Taynuilt, Argyll
Tel: 08663 333 · Fax: 08663 222

Perfect peace and quiet prevail at this Scottish Mansion standing on its own wooded promontory beneath the mighty peaks of Ben Cruachan. Surrounded by a world famous garden of rare shrubs, azaleas and rhododendrons, the elegant Drawing Room, Library and Dining Room overlook an incomparable panorama of island, loch and mountain scenery. Owners Mr & Mrs Robins aim is to provide Highland hospitality and good food in a relaxed atmosphere. For a while you can escape 20th century stress amidst the peace that is Ardanaiseig.

OPEN: **Easter to end October**
NO. ROOMS: **14 EN SUITE 14**
ROOM TELEPHONES: **Yes** TV IN ROOMS: **Yes**
PETS: **No** CHILDREN: **Over 8**
DISABLED: **Unsuitable**
LOCATION: **Turn off A85 at Taynuilt (nr Oban), Kilchrenan is on the B845**

SWIMMING POOL/HEALTH CLUB: **No**
CONFERENCE FACILITIES: **No**
PRICE GUIDE:
SINGLE: **£68 −£105 (incl Dinner)**
DOUBLE: **£136 −£210 (incl Dinner)**

Kildrummy Castle Hotel

Kildrummy, by Alford, Aberdeenshire A33 8RA
Tel: 09755 71288 · Fax: 09755 71345

Cross the threshold and you will feel you have stepped back in time. From the magnificent Great Hall with its elaborately ornate staircase to the quiet dignity of the public rooms and the elegant Dining Room where you will enjoy superb food and fine wines. Bedrooms are delightful, each individual in design and decor. This atmospheric old hotel overlooks the ruins of the 13th century castle from which it takes its name and is surrounded by the most beautiful gardens and grounds. Kildrummy is privately owned by Tom Hanna.

OPEN: **Closed January**
NO. ROOMS: **17** EN SUITE **17**
ROOM TELEPHONES: **Yes** TV IN ROOMS: **Yes**
PETS: **Yes** CHILDREN: **Yes**
DISABLED: **Unsuitable**
LOCATION: **Off A97 Huntly – Ballater road 35 miles west of Aberdeen**

SWIMMING POOL/HEALTH CLUB: **No**
CONFERENCE FACILITIES: **No**
PRICE GUIDE:
SINGLE: **£60**
DOUBLE: **£98/£110**

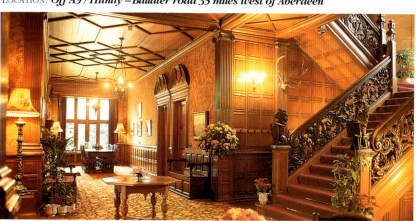

Knipoch Hotel
by Oban, Argyll
Tel: 08526 251 · Fax: 08526 249

Owned and operated by the Craig family, this attractive neo-Georgian hotel overlooks Loch Feochan. A combination of reproduction and antique furniture, log fires, fresh flowers, leather Chesterfields and fine panelling greet you on arrival. Delightful bedrooms all share superb loch views. Noted for the excellence of its cuisine based on local produce and daily changing menus and with an exceptional wine list of 350 bins, Knipoch is one of the finest hotels in Argyll.

OPEN: **Mid-February to Mid-November**
NO. ROOMS: **17** EN SUITE **17**
ROOM TELEPHONES: **Yes** TV IN ROOMS: **Yes**
PETS: **No** CHILDREN: **Yes**
DISABLED: **Unsuitable**

SWIMMING POOL/HEALTH CLUB: **No**
CONFERENCE FACILITIES: **No**
PRICE GUIDE:
SINGLE: **£56/£66**
DOUBLE: **£112/£130**

LOCATION: **Six miles south of Oban on A816 halfway along shores of Loch Feochan**

Ballathie House

Kinclaven by Stanley, Perthshire PH1 4QN
Tel: 025083 268 · Fax: 025083 396

Turning up the long drive leading to Ballathie adjectives like "imposing" and "majestic" spring to mind. Grand places can often be austere and cheerless, not so Ballathie, inside all is charm and elegance mirroring more gracious times. Supremely comfortable public rooms have splendid ceilings, fine fireplaces with log fires, and deep soft chairs and settees, with lovely views of garden and river. The finest of food is served in a quite stunning Dining Room and bedrooms are delightful, every one individual. This is a sportsmans paradise in quite glorious surroundings.

OPEN: *All year*
NO. ROOMS: *27* EN SUITE *27*
ROOM TELEPHONES: *Yes* TV IN ROOMS: *Yes*
PETS: *Yes* CHILDREN: *Yes*
DISABLED: *Yes*
LOCATION: *Off A9 two miles North of Perth through Stanley*

SWIMMING POOL/HEALTH CLUB: *No*
CONFERENCE FACILITIES:
Small Business Meetings
PRICE GUIDE:
SINGLE: *£50/£80* DOUBLE: *£86/£155*

The Kinlochbervie Hotel

Kinlochbervie, Sutherland IV27 4RP
Tel: 097182 275 · Fax: 097182 438

Mountains, lochs, rivers and oceans, plus the world's oldest rocks, form quite a contrast with this modern style hotel where high standards of comfort and cuisine are to be found. There is an excellent selection of wines and a large range of malt whiskies. Bedrooms are very well appointed and thoughtful extras, like hot water bottles, and at this, one of the most Northerly hotels in the U.K. you will be warmly welcomed by the owners Rex and Kate Neame.

OPEN: **March to December**
NO. ROOMS: **14** EN SUITE **14**
ROOM TELEPHONES: **Yes** TV IN ROOMS: **Yes**
PETS: **Yes** CHILDREN: **Yes**
DISABLED: **Unsuitable**
LOCATION: **Off the B801, turn right at Hotel Sign**

SWIMMING POOL/HEALTH CLUB: **No**
CONFERENCE FACILITIES: **No**
PRICE GUIDE:
SINGLE: **£45/£55**
DOUBLE: **£70/£90**

Leslie Castle

Leslie, By Insch, Aberdeen-shire AB5 6NX
Tel: 0464 20869 · Fax: 0464 21076

Straight out of a Walt Disney fairy tale, Leslie Castle with its turrets and towers has been most imaginatively restored by David and Leslie Leslie. The Castle is full of interest with its Baronial Hall, flag stoned floors and huge fireplace. Bedrooms are extremely comfortable and give the experience for a while of stepping back in time. Good food, fine wines and genuine Scottish hospitality here combine with the authentic atmosphere of a 17th century Castle to make your visit a memorable one.

OPEN: **All year**
NO. ROOMS: **4** EN SUITE **4**
ROOM TELEPHONES: **Yes** TV IN ROOMS: **Yes**
PETS: **No** CHILDREN: **Yes**
DISABLED: **Unsuitable**
LOCATION: **Two miles west of the B992 Auchleven/Leslie crossroads**

SWIMMING POOL/HEALTH CLUB: **No**
CONFERENCE FACILITIES:
Small Business Meetings up to 12
PRICE GUIDE:
SINGLE: **£77/£89** DOUBLE: **£103/£128**

Inver Lodge Hotel

Lochinver, Sutherland IV27 4IU
Tel: 05714 496 · Fax: 05714 395

This modern hotel, opened in 1988, stands in an elevated position with a backdrop of Suilven (the "Sugar Loaf") and Canisp mountains and looks towards the Hebrides. Every facility is provided in the exceptionally well equipped bedrooms with their six foot wide beds. Good food and fine wines can be enjoyed whilst admiring the dramatic scenery through large picture windows. There is a Shop, Sauna, Solarium and Snooker. Although it is the "great outdoors" which draws most people to this wild region, it is nice to know at the day's end that you also have the "great indoors".

OPEN: ***May 1st to end October***
NO. ROOMS: **20** EN SUITE **20**
ROOM TELEPHONES: **Yes** TV IN ROOMS: **Yes**
PETS: **Yes** CHILDREN: **Yes**
DISABLED: ***Unsuitable***
LOCATION: ***Through village on A835 and turn left after village hall***

SWIMMING POOL/HEALTH CLUB: **No**
CONFERENCE FACILITIES: **No**
PRICE GUIDE:
SINGLE: **£69/£78**
DOUBLE: **£106/£160**

Burts Hotel

Melrose, Roxburghshire
Tel: 089682 2285 · Fax: 089682 2870

I always find a visit to the Borders a refreshing change from the bedlam of life in most of Britain today. Blending with this historic region, Burts makes a pleasant base whether on business or holiday. Relax in attractive bedrooms which have every modern facility. Food, based on fresh local produce, is good Scottish with the accent on Taste of Scotland dishes, but also offers French haute cuisine and vegetarians are not forgotten. For lovers of history, Melrose is at the centre of a positive treasure house of places to visit. Your hosts, Graham and Anne Henderson will be pleased to help with your itinery.

OPEN: ***All year***
NO. ROOMS: **21** EN SUITE **21**
ROOM TELEPHONES: **Yes** TV IN ROOMS: **Yes**
PETS: **Yes** CHILDREN: **Yes**
DISABLED: **Unsuitable**
LOCATION: **In Melrose on Market Square**

SWIMMING POOL/HEALTH CLUB:
No
CONFERENCE FACILITIES:
No
PRICE GUIDE: SINGLE: **£42** DOUBLE: **£70**

Montgreenan Mansion House

Kilwinning, Ayrshire KA13 7QZ
Tel: 0294 57733 · Fax: 0294 85397

This imposing Mansion House dating from 1817 retains most of its impressive original 18th century features, marble fireplaces, elaborate ceilings and ornate plasterwork. Bedrooms include king-size beds, 4-posters and Jacuzzi baths. Traditional Scottish dishes feature prominently on the menus, and you can enjoy whisky and fine cigars specially chosen for the hotel. The world famous Golf Courses of Troon and Turnberry are a short drive away. Montgreenan is under the personal supervision of the owners Mr & Mrs Dobson and their family.

OPEN: **All year**
NO. ROOMS: **21** EN SUITE **21**
ROOM TELEPHONES: **Yes** TV IN ROOMS: **Yes**
PETS: **By arrangement** CHILDREN: **Yes**
DISABLED: **Unsuitable**
LOCATION: **4 miles north of Irvine off A736 Glasgow – Irvine road**

SWIMMING POOL/HEALTH CLUB: **No**
CONFERENCE FACILITIES:
Small Business Meetings up to 100
PRICE GUIDE:
SINGLE: **From £70** DOUBLE: **From £140**

Udny Arms Hotel

Main Street, Newburgh, Aberdeenshire AB41 0BC
Tel: 03586 89444 · Fax: 03586 89012

Relaxed informality in an ambience of comfort and congeniality is the aim of the Craig family who own and operate this fine Victorian Hotel. Overlooking the Ythan Estuary and the Golf Course, the Udny Arms is a hostelry noted for good food, and for which they have received numerous accolades. You have a choice for dining between the charming elegance of the Dining Room or the excellent value Bistro. Try their famous sticky toffee pudding. With its delightful bedrooms, this renowned hotel continues to dispense hospitality as it has done for over 100 years.

OPEN: ***All year***
NO. ROOMS: ***26*** EN SUITE ***26***
ROOM TELEPHONES: ***Yes*** TV IN ROOMS: ***Yes***
PETS: ***Yes*** CHILDREN: ***Yes***
DISABLED: ***Unsuitable***

SWIMMING POOL/HEALTH CLUB: ***No***
CONFERENCE FACILITIES: ***Residential 20 to 125 Theatre Style***
PRICE GUIDE:
SINGLE: ***£57*** DOUBLE: ***£75***

The Lodge on the Loch

Onich, Near Fort William, Inverness-shire PH33 6RY
Tel: 08553 237/8 · Fax: 08553 463

Situated in the "heart of the Highlands" on the banks of Loch Linnhe, the hotel commands a panorama of mountain and loch scenery. Soft colour co-ordinated fabrics convey a pleasing air to public rooms and bedrooms alike. "Taste of Scotland" dishes are a feature of the interesting menus as are vegetarian dishes, wholefoods and home baking. The influence of the Gulf Stream can be seen in the palms and wild rhododendrons which abound locally. This attractive hotel, owned by the Young family makes an ideal base for touring the Western Highlands.

OPEN: **Feb to early Nov & Xmas & New Year**
NO. ROOMS: **20** EN SUITE **18**
ROOM TELEPHONES: **Yes** TV IN ROOMS: **Yes**
PETS: **Yes** CHILDREN: **Yes**
DISABLED: **Yes**
LOCATION: **Off A82 five miles north of Glencoe**

SWIMMING POOL/HEALTH CLUB:
At own nearby Club
CONFERENCE FACILITIES: **No**
PRICE GUIDE:
SINGLE: **From £50** DOUBLE: **£99**

Cringletie House

Peebles, EH45 8PL
Tel: 07213 233 · Fax: 07213 244

This impressive Scottish Baronial Mansion is owned and operated by Stan and Aileen Maguire. All bedrooms are tastefully appointed with superb views. Particularly noteworthy is the handsome dark panelled Drawing Room with its marble fireplace and painted ceiling. You can enjoy pre-dinner drinks in the Library Bar with its log fire and sample delicious freshly cooked food, the kitchen being under the supervision of Mrs Maguire. Cringletie is ideally situated for touring the historic Border country and convenient for Edinburgh.

OPEN: *Early march to January 1st*
NO. ROOMS: *13* EN SUITE *13*
ROOM TELEPHONES: *Yes* TV IN ROOMS: *Yes*
PETS: *Yes* CHILDREN: *Yes*
DISABLED: *Unsuitable*

SWIMMING POOL/HEALTH CLUB:
No
CONFERENCE FACILITIES:
No
PRICE GUIDE: SINGLE: *£47.50* DOUBLE: *£86*

LOCATION: *2½ miles North of Peebles on A703, twenty miles from Edinburgh*

Parkland House Hotel

St Leonards Bank, Perth PH2 8EB
Tel: 0738 22451 · Fax: 0738 22046

Perth City's latest small luxury hotel opened in 1991. A "Country House in Town" Parklands is owned by Allan & Pat Deeson (see also under Cleish) who have created an oasis of good living overlooking the attractive park. Fine panelling, elaborate cornices and meticulous attention to detail make this a must for business or pleasure. Bedrooms are luxurious and beautifully appointed whilst in the elegant Restaurant delicious food imaginatively presented by a top French Chef emphasises "Taste of Scotland" specialities.

OPEN: **All year**
NO. ROOMS: **14** EN SUITE **14**
ROOM TELEPHONES: **Yes** TV IN ROOMS: **Yes**
PETS: **Yes** CHILDREN: **Yes**
DISABLED: **Yes**
LOCATION: **Next to main line railway station**

SWIMMING POOL/HEALTH CLUB: **No**
CONFERENCE FACILITIES:
Small Business Meetings up to 16
PRICE GUIDE:
SINGLE: **£70/£80** DOUBLE: **£85/£125**

Murrayshall House

Scone, Perthshire PH2 7PH
Tel: 0738 51171 · Fax: 0738 52595

This beautiful Country House Hotel set in 300 acres of parkland with its own Golf Course would be hard to better. Accolades for Restaurant of the Year and Chef of the Year give a hint of the gastronomic delights that await you in one of the most attractive Restaurants it has been my privilege to eat in. Original 16th and 17th century oil paintings grace the walls, there is an open fire and a musician plays at dinner. Decor throughout is imaginative and furnishings are luxurious, the bedrooms are particularly appealing with everything the discerning guest could wish. Staff are welcoming and courteous.

OPEN: *All year*
NO. ROOMS: *19* EN SUITE *19*
ROOM TELEPHONES: *Yes* TV IN ROOMS: *Yes*
PETS: *Yes* CHILDREN: *Over 10*
DISABLED: *Unsuitable*
LOCATION: *Off the A94 Couper Angus Road from Perth*

SWIMMING POOL/HEALTH CLUB: *No*
CONFERENCE FACILITIES:
Up to 40 delegates
PRICE GUIDE: SINGLE: *£75* DOUBLE: *£110*
(1992 Tariff)

Pine Trees Hotel

Strathview Terrace, Pitlochry, Perthshire PH16 5QR
Tel: 0796 2121 · Fax: 0796 2460

A comprehensive re-furbishment programme has recently been completed at this Scottish Mansion owned and operated by Mr & Mrs MacClellan and family, from whom you will receive a real Highland welcome. A homely atmosphere prevails here with pleasing public rooms and well appointed bedrooms, enhanced by fine panelling and other quality period features. You won't need a bank loan to stay here either, prices are very reasonable. Just minutes away from the renowned Festival Theatre, the Pine Trees makes a good base for exploring the Scottish Highlands.

OPEN: ***Mid-March to early January***
NO. ROOMS: **18** EN SUITE **17**
ROOM TELEPHONES: **Yes** TV IN ROOMS: **Yes**
PETS: **By arrangement** CHILDREN: **Yes**
DISABLED: **Unsuitable**

SWIMMING POOL/HEALTH CLUB:
No
CONFERENCE FACILITIES:
No
PRICE GUIDE: SINGLE: **£46** DOUBLE: **£84**

LOCATION: ***Through town coming from South. Hotel signed after the Old Smiddy Rest***

The Haven Hotel

Plockton, Ross-shire IV52 8TW
Tel: 059984 223

If Plockton is known as "the jewel of The Highlands" then the Haven is assuredly "the jewel of Plockton"! This delightful small hotel is run with genuine warmth and friendliness by Marjorie Nichols and John Graham. Comfortable bedrooms are very well appointed whilst in the pleasant candle-lit Dining Room you will enjoy Scottish cooking at its best. For value for money it would be difficult to beat The Haven. You could hardly do better than to make it your base for touring this magnificent part of the Western Highlands.

OPEN: *February 1st to December 20th*
NO. ROOMS: *13* EN SUITE *13*
ROOM TELEPHONES: *Yes* TV IN ROOMS: *Yes*
PETS: *Yes* CHILDREN: *Over 10*
DISABLED: *Unsuitable*
LOCATION: *Six miles North East of Kyle of Localsh on Loch Carron*

SWIMMING POOL/HEALTH CLUB: *No*
CONFERENCE FACILITIES: *No*
PRICE GUIDE:
SINGLE: *£44/£51 (incl Dinner)*
DOUBLE: *£88/£102 (incl Dinner)*

The Eddrachilles Hotel

Badcall Bay, Scourie, Sutherland IV27 4TH
Tel: 0971 502080 · Fax: 0971 502477

It would be difficult to imagine a more magnificent view than the one commanded by this small hotel overlooking as it does the bejewelled islands of Badcall Bay. Spotless bedrooms have every modern convenience and home cooking is served in the pleasant Dining Room with its exposed stone walls and original flagstone floors. Mr and Mrs Wood are your welcoming hosts in this mature lovers paradise.

OPEN: **March to October**
NO. ROOMS: **11** EN SUITE **11**
ROOM TELEPHONES: **Yes** TV IN ROOMS: **Yes**
PETS: **No** CHILDREN: **Over 3**
DISABLED: **Unsuitable**
LOCATION: **Off A834 two miles south of Scourie**

SWIMMING POOL/HEALTH CLUB: **No**
CONFERENCE FACILITIES: **No**
PRICE GUIDE:
SINGLE: **£40/£45**
DOUBLE: **£60/£70**

Manor Park

Skelmorlie, Ayrshire PA17 5HE
Tel: 0475 520832 · Fax: 0475 520832

This fine house has an interesting history, having been the scene of a wartime meeting between Churchill & Eisenhower. Situated in what has to be one of the finest gardens in Ayrshire overlooking the Firth of Clyde, the house has a number of unusual features: the Adam style Hall with its elaborate ceiling and plasterwork and a simply stunning ornate Cupola surrounding a magnificent oak staircase. Lovely views of garden or sea are obtained from the bedrooms. Under the supervision of resident proprietor Frederick Williams.

OPEN: **All year**
NO. ROOMS: **23** EN SUITE **23**
ROOM TELEPHONES: **Yes** TV IN ROOMS: **Yes**
PETS: **By arrangement** CHILDREN: **Yes**
DISABLED: **Yes**
LOCATION: **Off A78 two miles North of Langs**

SWIMMING POOL: **No**
CONFERENCE FACILITIES:
Business Meetings up to 100
PRICE GUIDE:
SINGLE: **£45/£65** DOUBLE: **£70/£120**

Dalmunzie House

Spittal o'Glenshee, Blairgowrie, Perthshire PH10 7QG
Tel: 025085 224 · Fax: 025085 225

Nestling in solitary splendour within its own 6,000 acre estate against a mountain backdrop, this turreted hotel is owned and operated by the Winton family. Log fires, good Scottish fare, charming comfortable bedrooms all make for a pleasurable stay in winter or summer. With too many sporting facilities to list, you will find in Dalmunzie House a cheerful family atmosphere offering real value for money.

OPEN: ***December 28th to October 31st***
NO. ROOMS: **18** EN SUITE **16**
ROOM TELEPHONES: **No** TV IN ROOMS: **No**
PETS: **Yes** CHILDREN: **Yes**
DISABLED: **Yes**

SWIMMING POOL/HEALTH CLUB: **No**
CONFERENCE FACILITIES: **No**
PRICE GUIDE:
SINGLE: **£44/£50**
DOUBLE: **£66/£82**

LOCATION: ***18 miles north of Blairgowrie, left at Spittal o'Glenshee***

St. Andrews Old Course Hotel

St. Andrews, Fife KY16 9SP
Tel: 0334 74371 · Fax: 0334 77668

It would be easy to run out of superlatives in trying to describe this fabulous hotel. Overlooking the world famous Royal and Ancient Clubhouse, it has interiors of dazzling opulence with its superb panelled Library, antiques and original works of art. Exquisite bedrooms and stunning suites are the last word in luxury with magnificent marbled bathrooms. In the matchless elegance of the main Restaurant, classically inspired original dishes are presented with great flair. "The Spa" is one of the finest Leisure Complexes I have seen in the UK Truly a hotel "fit for the Gods".

OPEN: *All year*
NO. ROOMS: *125* EN SUITE *125*
ROOM TELEPHONES: *Yes* TV IN ROOMS: *Yes*
PETS: *By arrangement* CHILDREN: *Yes*
DISABLED: *Yes*

SWIMMING POOL/HEALTH CLUB: *Yes*
CONFERENCE FACILITIES:
Theatre style 180/200: Classroom 150
PRICE GUIDE: SINGLE: *£150/£205*
DOUBLE: *£210/£250* SUITES: *£275/£350*

Dryburgh Abbey Hotel

St Boswells, Roxburghshire TD6 0RQ
Tel: 0835 22261 · Fax: 0835 23945

Apart from its exterior, regular visitors to this famous Borders hotel simply will not recognise it. A total transformation by new owners the Grose family (see also under Thurlestone, Devon) has resulted in the most luxurious hotel in the area. Beautifully designed and furnished bedrooms have every modern facility. Situated on the banks of the world famous River Tweed, guests can admire the tranquil setting whilst dining in the elegant surroundings of the Tweed Restaurant. In an area where quality hotels are thin on the ground, Dryburgh Abbey takes its place amongst Scotland's finest.

OPEN: **All year**
NO. ROOMS: **28** EN SUITE **28**
ROOM TELEPHONES: **Yes** TV IN ROOMS: **Yes**
PETS: **Yes** CHILDREN: **Yes**
DISABLED: **Yes**

SWIMMING POOL/HEALTH CLUB: **No**
CONFERENCE FACILITIES:
Up to 150 Theatre Style
PRICE GUIDE:
SINGLE: **£50/£80** DOUBLE: **£100/£160**

Chapeltoun House

Stewarton, Ayreshire KA3 3ED
Tel: 0560 82696 · Fax: 0560 85100

A wealth of oak panelling and the cheerful welcome of a log fire greet you on arrival at this former gentlemans residence. Award winning chefs present interesting dishes utilising fresh produce and you can dine in a choice of two oak panelled Dining Rooms whilst admiring the lovely garden. All bedrooms are comfortable and furnished in traditional style with some fine antique pieces. Royal Troon and Turnberry golf courses are nearby. Your hosts, Colin and Graham McKenzie.

OPEN: **All year**

NO. ROOMS: **8** EN SUITE **8**

ROOM TELEPHONES: **Yes** TV IN ROOMS: **Yes**

PETS: **By arrangement** CHILDREN: **Over 12**

DISABLED: **Unsuitable**

SWIMMING POOL/HEALTH CLUB: **No**

CONFERENCE FACILITIES:

Director level up to 20

PRICE GUIDE:

SINGLE: **£69/£84** DOUBLE: **£99/£129**

LOCATION: **Through Stewarton on A735, 2nd right after viaduct onto B769, Hotel two miles**

Park Lodge Hotel

32 Park Terrace, Stirling FK8 2JS
Tel: 0786 74862

This elegant Georgian "country house in town" overlooks Stirling Castle and the Golf Course. Owned and operated by Mrs Marquetty, Park Lodge is beautifully arranged with superb antiques, fine paintings and rich drapes, all set against a background of baroque panels, elaborate cornices and mouldings. The individuality of the public rooms are reflected in the bedrooms and excellent bathrooms. A recent addition is the elegant conference room which can accommodate 100 delegates in style.

OPEN: **All year**
NO. ROOMS: **9** EN SUITE **9**
ROOM TELEPHONES: **Yes** TV IN ROOMS: **Yes**
PETS: **Yes** CHILDREN: **Yes**
DISABLED: **Yes**

SWIMMING POOL/HEALTH CLUB: **No**
CONFERENCE FACILITIES:
Up to 100 Theatre Style
PRICE GUIDE:
SINGLE: **£45/£60** DOUBLE: **£65/£90**

Port-an-Eilean House Hotel

Strathtummel, Nr Pitlochry, Perthshire PH16 5RU
Tel: 08824 233

Owners Gordon & Evelyn Hallewell will welcome you most warmly to their tranquil hotel in its lochside setting. Originally built as a sporting lodge for the 6th Duke of Atholl, Port-an-Eilean is now a comfortable small hotel offering good food in a relaxed atmosphere and an unlimited supply of "peace and quiet". Superb views of the surrounding mountains and loch are obtained from the Sun Lounge and there is an interesting collection of paintings, the work of contemporary Scottish artists.

OPEN: *May 1st to early October*
NO. ROOMS: *8* EN SUITE *8*
ROOM TELEPHONES: *No* TV IN ROOMS: *No*
PETS: *Yes* CHILDREN: *Yes*
DISABLED: *Unsuitable*
LOCATION: *Nine miles west of Pitlochry on B8019*

SWIMMING POOL/HEALTH CLUB:
No
CONFERENCE FACILITIES:
No
PRICE GUIDE: SINGLE: *£36* DOUBLE: *£60*

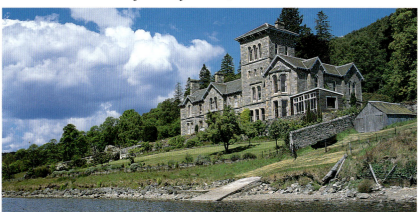

Index

(Hotels listed alphabetically by name)

Index   260

ORDER: CHARISMA PUBLICATIONS
12 Victoria Quay, Nr Truro, South Cornwall TR1 1ST

Date_____Please mail_____(Number of copies) of your

"Connoisseurs Choice" 1992, to: Mr/Mrs/Miss_____

Address _____

_____Post Code_____

To any UK address –   Retail price £12.95 (add £3.15 for 1 copy, £4.10 for 2 to 3 copies)
To USA –   Retail price $21.95 (add $6.09 for 1 copy, $21.98 for 2 copies)
To Canada –   Retail price $24.95 (add $6.88 for 1 copy, $24.83 for 2 copies)
Rest of the world   Add £3.55 post & packing for 1 copy.
        All overseas Cheques to be drawn on U.K. Bank. Allow 21 days for delivery.

I enclose £_____ to cover cost of _____copy/copies.

Cheques to be made payable to **Charisma Publications**

ORDER: CHARISMA PUBLICATIONS
12 Victoria Quay, Nr Truro, South Cornwall TR1 1ST

Date_____Please mail_____(Number of copies) of your

"Connoisseurs Choice" 1992, to: Mr/Mrs/Miss_____

Address _____

_____Post Code_____

To any UK address –   Retail price £12.95 (add £3.15 for 1 copy, £4.10 for 2 to 3 copies)
To USA –   Retail price $21.95 (add $6.09 for 1 copy, $21.98 for 2 copies)
To Canada –   Retail price $24.95 (add $6.88 for 1 copy, $24.83 for 2 copies)
Rest of the world   Add £3.55 post & packing for 1 copy.
        All overseas Cheques to be drawn on U.K. Bank. Allow 21 days for delivery.

I enclose £_____ to cover cost of _____copy/copies.

Cheques to be made payable to **Charisma Publications**

ORDER: CHARISMA PUBLICATIONS
12 Victoria Quay, Nr Truro, South Cornwall TR1 1ST

Date_____Please mail_____(Number of copies) of your

"Connoisseurs Choice" 1992, to: Mr/Mrs/Miss_____

Address _____

_____Post Code_____

To any UK address –   Retail price £12.95 (add £3.15 for 1 copy, £4.10 for 2 to 3 copies)
To USA –   Retail price $21.95 (add $6.09 for 1 copy, $21.98 for 2 copies)
To Canada –   Retail price $24.95 (add $6.88 for 1 copy, $24.83 for 2 copies)
Rest of the world   Add £3.55 post & packing for 1 copy.
        All overseas Cheques to be drawn on U.K. Bank. Allow 21 days for delivery.

I enclose £_____ to cover cost of _____copy/copies.

Cheques to be made payable to **Charisma Publications**

To obtain your own personal copy of this book –
please complete reverse side of this slip.

To obtain your own personal copy of this book –
please complete reverse side of this slip.

To obtain your own personal copy of this book –
please complete reverse side of this slip.

ORDER: CHARISMA PUBLICATIONS
          12 Victoria Quay, Nr Truro, South Cornwall TR1 1ST

Date_____Please mail_____(Number of copies) of your

"Connoisseurs Choice" 1992, to: Mr/Mrs/Miss_____

Address _____

_____Post Code_____

To any UK address –   Retail price £12.95 (add £3.15 for 1 copy, £4.10 for 2 to 3 copies)
To USA –   Retail price $21.95 (add $6.09 for 1 copy, $21.98 for 2 copies)
To Canada –   Retail price $24.95 (add $6.88 for 1 copy, $24.83 for 2 copies)
Rest of the world   Add £3.55 post & packing for 1 copy.
          All overseas Cheques to be drawn on U.K. Bank. Allow 21 days for delivery.

I enclose £_____ to cover cost of _____copy/copies.

Cheques to be made payable to **Charisma Publications**

ORDER: CHARISMA PUBLICATIONS
          12 Victoria Quay, Nr Truro, South Cornwall TR1 1ST

Date_____Please mail_____(Number of copies) of your

"Connoisseurs Choice" 1992, to: Mr/Mrs/Miss_____

Address _____

_____Post Code_____

To any UK address –   Retail price £12.95 (add £3.15 for 1 copy, £4.10 for 2 to 3 copies)
To USA –   Retail price $21.95 (add $6.09 for 1 copy, $21.98 for 2 copies)
To Canada –   Retail price $24.95 (add $6.88 for 1 copy, $24.83 for 2 copies)
Rest of the world   Add £3.55 post & packing for 1 copy.
          All overseas Cheques to be drawn on U.K. Bank. Allow 21 days for delivery.

I enclose £_____ to cover cost of _____copy/copies.

Cheques to be made payable to **Charisma Publications**

ORDER: CHARISMA PUBLICATIONS
          12 Victoria Quay, Nr Truro, South Cornwall TR1 1ST

Date_____Please mail_____(Number of copies) of your

"Connoisseurs Choice" 1992, to: Mr/Mrs/Miss_____

Address _____

_____Post Code_____

To any UK address –   Retail price £12.95 (add £3.15 for 1 copy, £4.10 for 2 to 3 copies)
To USA –   Retail price $21.95 (add $6.09 for 1 copy, $21.98 for 2 copies)
To Canada –   Retail price $24.95 (add $6.88 for 1 copy, $24.83 for 2 copies)
Rest of the world   Add £3.55 post & packing for 1 copy.
          All overseas Cheques to be drawn on U.K. Bank. Allow 21 days for delivery.

I enclose £_____ to cover cost of _____copy/copies.

Cheques to be made payable to **Charisma Publications**

To obtain your own personal copy of this book –
please complete reverse side of this slip.

To obtain your own personal copy of this book –
please complete reverse side of this slip.

To obtain your own personal copy of this book –
please complete reverse side of this slip.